Cryptocommunism

Theory Redux series

Series editor: Laurent de Sutter

Published Titles

Mark Alizart, *Cryptocommunism*

Armen Avanessian, *Future Metaphysics*

Franco Berardi, *The Second Coming*

Alfie Bown, *The Playstation Dreamworld*

Laurent de Sutter, *Narcocapitalism*

Roberto Esposito, *Persons and Things*

Graham Harman, *Immaterialism*

Helen Hester, *Xenofeminism*

Srećko Horvat, *The Radicality of Love*

Dominic Pettman, *Infinite Distraction*

Nick Srnicek, *Platform Capitalism*

Cryptocommunism

Mark Alizart

Translated by Robin Mackay

polity

Polity Press
65 Bridge Street
Cambridge CB2 1UR, UK

Polity Press
101 Station Landing
Suite 300
Medford, MA 02155, USA

ISBN-13: 978-1-5095-3857-7
ISBN-13: 978-1-5095-3858-4 (pb)

A catalogue record for this book is available from the British Library.

Library of Congress Cataloging-in-Publication Data
Names: Alizart, Mark, author.
Title: Cryptocommunism / Mark Alizart ; translated by Robin Mackay.
Other titles: Cryptocommunisme. English
Description: Cambridge, UK ; Medford, MA : Polity Press, [2020] | Series: Theory redux series | Includes bibliographical references and index. | Summary: "The communist manifesto for the age of Bitcoin"-- Provided by publisher.
Identifiers: LCCN 2020004522 (print) | LCCN 2020004523 (ebook) | ISBN 9781509538577 (hardback) | ISBN 9781509538584 (paperback) | ISBN 9781509538591 (epub)
Subjects: LCSH: Communism and technology. | Cryptocurrencies--Philosophy. | Value--Philosophy.
Classification: LCC HX543.5 .A4513 2020 (print) | LCC HX543.5 (ebook) | DDC 332.4--dc23
LC record available at https://lccn.loc.gov/2020004522
LC ebook record available at https://lccn.loc.gov/2020004523

Typeset in 12.5/15 Adobe Garamond by
Servis Filmsetting Ltd, Stockport, Cheshire
Printed and bound in Great Britain by CPI Group (UK) Ltd, Croydon

For further information on Polity, visit our website: politybooks.com

Communism = Soviets + Electricity
Lenin

Contents

Acknowledgements

My thanks first of all to Laurent de Sutter, for the trust he placed in me by accepting this book into his collection. I would also like to express my gratitude to John Thompson and Polity Press, to my translator Robin Mackay, and to the readers who agreed to reread my manuscript and helped guide my thinking: Brune Compagnon-Janin, Anthony Masure, Aliocha Imhoff and Kantuta Quiros, Mathieu Potte-Bonneville, as well as Odile Lakomski-Laguerre, Jacques Favier and Adli Takkal Bataille.

Introduction: The Institution of Liberty

Cryptocurrencies are often deemed 'revolution-ary' and, indeed, Bitcoin's manifesto shares striking similarities with the most prominent revolutions in history. Satoshi Nakamoto's vision that it is possible to trade without bankers as intermediaries cannot but remind us of Martin Luther's claim that believers can entertain a direct relationship with God without priests as interme-diaries, which in 1517 kickstarted the Protestant Reformation. It has a similar feel to the declara-tions of Oliver Cromwell, George Washington and Maximilien de Robespierre, according to which the people can govern themselves without princes as intermediaries, declarations that gave rise to the great political revolutions.

Obviously, the Bitcoin 'White Paper' doesn't tell us how to obtain eternal life like the Reformation did, and the petty calculations of small investors worried about their savings seem to have little in common with the struggle for liberty, so one might well doubt whether any of this goes beyond a vague resonance, and whether Bitcoin really promises the same kind of disruptions as those earlier revolutions. But it would be a great mistake to overlook cryptocurrencies because they are just about 'money'. Finance is anything but trivial. The economy is not only a fundamental aspect of our societies; in some senses it is the continuation of the religious and political spheres by other means.

Holy communion wafers are shaped like coins because originally both were cast in the same moulds.[1] The first 'central banks' in history were founded in reformed countries; financial engineering required 'trust', above all, trust being just another word for 'faith'.[2] By placing faith (*fides*) and guilt at the centre of religious life, Protestantism allowed associates who trusted one other (*con-fide*) to give each other 'credit' (*crede*, 'to believe') for their debts (moral as well as financial). It was a Protestant, John Law, who introduced the first paper money into France at the beginning of the eighteenth century.[3] And it is also the Protestant concept of faith, in the sense that implies trust and letting go, and therefore *being free*, that supported the construction of liberal democracies and allowed them to emancipate themselves from monarchy.

In fact, Satoshi's invention, insofar as it also deals in trust and faith, is a substantial and worthy heir to the theological political history of the West that runs from the Reformation to liberal democracy. It may even represent its fulfilment, for whereas reformation and revolution were based in a subjective concept of faith, Bitcoin is an *algorithm* of faith. Because it allows mathematical emancipation from 'trusted third parties', it is a machine for producing faith and liberty.[4]

This having been said, revolutions are also plagued by misconceptions, and the cryptorevolution is no exception; Cryptocurrency 'fanatics' – we use the word advisedly, since it is indeed a new religion and a new party – may be in for a disappointment regarding their beliefs. The cryptorevolution might spell the end of the international financial system as we know it, but it won't end all misery and injustice, neither will it give birth to a brave new world of empowered individuals freed from paying taxes and obeying the law – the story that a great many libertarian prophets, alt-right bitcoiners and cryptocultists like to tell. If revolutions of the past teach us something, it is that emancipation, freedom and liberty have a very special way of coming up with new obligations and even, sometimes, woes.

Certainly, during the Middle Ages peasants gathered around Reformation gurus such as Thomas Müntzer, who had deduced from Luther's theses that it was now possible to live free of all moral and clerical authority. And there were revolutionary *enragés* who believed that their newly gained freedom gave them the right to cut off as many heads as they wanted, especially those raised above their own. Eventually though, all of them would discover sooner rather than later that they were mistaken about the deeper meaning of the Reformation and the Revolution. Protestantism was to introduce even more rigour into religion than Catholicism, to the point where Protestants would end up being known as 'Puritans'. Priests were abolished, cathedrals, altars, incense and Church Latin destroyed, replaced by a religious practice that did away with all visible signs only to become all the more ascetic, demanding to be observed at all times and in every aspect of secular life. Similarly, democracy would prove to be even more complex and convoluted than the *ancien régime*. The princes were cast out, only for bureaucracy to run rampant, with swarms of civil servants and lawbooks thicker than the dictionary and telephone book combined.

Now, it might be argued that the return of Church and State following the Reformation, and the liberal revolutions that had attempted to destroy them, means that they failed at what they set out to do and that the real, proper revolution is yet to come.[5] But the truth is that this return was a feature, not a bug. Luther didn't want to overthrow the law of God, he wanted to fulfil it; Rousseau didn't want the rule of nature to replace the rule of men, he wanted to ensure that the rule of men would be duly observed and carried out. In fact, they had both understood that liberty is paradoxically the best way to enforce the word of God and the rule of men, because ultimately it consists not in being free from all laws, but in freely imposing laws upon oneself, as the word 'autonomy' clearly suggests: a 'law' (*nomos*) imposed upon 'oneself' (*auto*).

Liberty is not a whim. It is an institution. It relies on institutions and it creates institutions. The same can be said about Satoshi's project. Bitcoin seeks to restore trust, not to destroy it. It seeks to restore institutions we can believe in, not burn them to the ground. It wants to make this society liveable. And in a very compelling sense, it does so in the same way as the Reformation and the revolutions did: by replacing old institutions with new ones, which are more robust only because they are *chosen* institutions. Bitcoin frees us by allowing us to impose chains upon ourselves, as the appropriately named *blockchain* clearly indicates.

Thus, there is no doubt that cryptocurrencies will bring with them a new wind of change, spreading freedom across the world; but there are reasons to believe this will happen not in the way dreamt of by the eager children of the Tea Party, but by subjecting our lives to a new church and a new state yet more ascetic than Luther's Reformation, more rigorous than Rousseau's Republic. The theological-political regime of crypto will not be 'cryptoanarchism';

quite the contrary, it will be a regime that will impose a new law on us, a new *common* law, more austere than liberal laws, thus more like a regime that too deemed itself to be revolutionary in its time, even if it didn't succeed in bringing about the revolution its believers had hoped for: namely, communism – or, more precisely, *cryptocommunism.*

Part I

Government of People, Administration of Things

I

A State without Statism

In crypto circles, communism often figures as everything crypto is not: statist, centralizing, planned and totalitarian, where crypto sees itself as decentralized, liberal and emancipatory. But who was the first person to ask how one could do without the state and its representatives, before Satoshi Nakamoto, Ayn Rand or Friedrich Hayek? None other than Karl Marx.

Marx was a lover of freedom, and his ambition as a philosopher and politician was precisely to find a way to safeguard freedom. After all, he belonged to a generation that had witnessed the heist pulled off by the business bourgeoisie so as to benefit from the French Revolution. He had seen upstarts reclaiming all their privileges off the backs of the populace that had brought them to power. He hated these fake aristocrats who had hijacked public wealth with the alibi of advancing the people's cause. He wanted to prevent these new masters from putting the genie of the Enlightenment ideal of emancipation back into the bottle. Marx was, in essence, the first to seek to radicalize revolution, and even reformation. A great admirer of Luther, he thought that just as Luther had demolished the clergy, so it was his responsibility to demolish the state. What he had in mind under the name of communism was essentially that 'public power' would lose its 'political character', as he wrote in the *Communist Party Manifesto*,[1] the aim being to ensure that 'the government of men gives way to the administration of things', to paraphrase his sidekick Friedrich Engels[2] – upon which, '[i]n place of the old bourgeois society . . . we shall have an association, in which the free development of each is the condition for the free development of all'.[3]

These are words that could have been penned by the author of the *Crypto Anarchist Manifesto*. And that's no coincidence. At first, the socialist movement was almost indistinguishable from the anarchist movement led by Pierre-Joseph

Proudhon, Mikhail Bakunin and Louis Blanc. It really only differed on one point, albeit a crucial one, and one that interests us particularly in that it allows us to understand the link between communism and the blockchain: Marx believed that the destatization of society had to be accompanied by some other kind of organization or protocol, otherwise the same causes would generate the same effects all over again: private forces would take advantage of public weakness to confiscate common property and the state would rise up again, even stronger, from the ashes, as the crushing of the Commune in 1870–1 had proved.

It's not so much that Marx didn't trust the market to replace the state (all indications are that it's quite capable of doing so); he did not trust the market's ability to remain a market if left to itself. Marx's very original thesis is that, the market would turn once more into a state. Indeed, the state doesn't 'oppress' entrepreneurs, as is their usual complaint. Quite the contrary: it is something they create. It is invented by capitalists in order to protect their private property, to advance their interests and to deter the growth of competition. In other words, the state is never just a dominant private interest disguising itself as the public interest.[4] It is a fully fledged actor in the market.

Paradoxically, this point makes Marx much more closely affiliated with the libertarians than we usually think. For libertarians also believe that the markets are manipulated by politicians and that therefore they must be liberated from this political control so that they can become efficient again. Destroying the state means preventing the mechanism whereby the market secretes the state like an oyster secretes a pearl. So libertarians don't simply want to suppress the state, any more than Marx does. On the contrary: since politics tends always to rise again from its ashes, Hayek, for example, advocated that governments be placed under the supervision of higher structures, capable of imposing rules of free competition that must apply to all without distinction.

The only difference between Marx and libertarians is the structure that is to be responsible for regulating the market. For Hayek, it was to be an unelected 'council of wise men' presiding over executive and legislative power and which, in addition to being responsible for regulating the market, would also take pride in giving its opinion on moral issues (since the people must be 'educated' to freedom, according to the Austrian thinker, who never hid his sympathy for fascism despite his proclaimed love of freedom – or more paradoxically, because of it). For Marx, it was to be 'popular councils' endowed with the same powers (what would become the 'Soviets' in Lenin's era). But even this doesn't provide much ground for differentiating between Marxists and libertarians – or, at least, they failed equally: councils of elders and popular councils alike failed to do their job.

Bakunin had predicted that Marx's passion for political organization would lead him to replace the bourgeois state with a 'red bureaucracy' that would be just as bad, and ultimately he was proved right. Under the yoke of Lenin and then Stalin, the fearsome fantasy of a 'dictatorship of the proletariat' morphed into the infamous 'Party', a real state within the state that betrayed the trust of the proletarians it was supposed to serve; a tool of 'democratic centralism' in which centralism always trumped democracy.

But it is no unfair exaggeration to say that libertarianism has scarcely been more successful than Marxism in convincing people of the effectiveness of its system. Hayek's recommendations have been followed around the world as, in what is known as 'neoliberalism', technocratic institutions everywhere have supplanted the general will: what are called 'central banks' (institutions against which libertarians are constantly railing, not realizing that they themselves invented them!), but also the International Monetary Fund and the World Bank (all the presidents and governors of which are unelected).[5] Not to mention 'Supreme Courts' (whose judges are also unelected) and various 'Central Intelligence Agencies' (whose leaders, once more, are unelected). The problem with all these institutions is that the personalities who head them up, without any popular supervision, must therefore be *appointed* by the most loyal and devoted representatives of the oligarchy. In the end, Hayek and his buddies in the neoliberal cadre of the Mont Pelerin Society will have served as nothing but useful idiots for big business (that is, unless they were in cahoots from the very start).

But then, if neither popular councils nor unelected technocrats can overcome the dysfunctions of the market, who on earth can? That's where Bitcoin comes in, precisely because it seems to provide a solution to this impasse. It seems to be the missing piece that communism needed in order to carry out its 'organized destruction' of the state.

2

Cybernetics and Governmentality

Norbert Wiener, the father of cybernetics, was one of the first to have understood, as early as the 1950s, that information technology offered a solution to the problem of democratic governance. Indeed, the very word 'cybernetics' harbours a reference to the 'science of good government' (*kubernetes*, the Greek word from which *cybernetics* is derived, means 'steersman'). According to Wiener, a society could be described just like any other system that seeks equilibrium ('homeostasis') through positive feedback loops – so it had to be optimally controlled by automated and decentralized algorithms, just as a body's vital functions are controlled by the nervous system without any conscious intervention on our part.[1]

A certain persistent rumour has it that cybernetics was right wing, with cyberneticians so fulsome in their praise of both an antidemocratic form of control and a liberal system of self-regulation. But no such stance appears in the work of Wiener, who rejected both Stalinism and hyperliberalism (indeed, he was forced to remove his comparison of the two from the second edition of his book in order to appease McCarthyist communist hunters). In fact, like the entire generation of scientists who were part of the 'Manhattan Project', Wiener was haunted by anxiety that the public good might fall into the hands of some Doctor Strangelove, whether communist or capitalist. In this sense, his insistence on automation and decentralization is akin to Marx's obsession with a state protected from human greed and folly.

Not by chance, it was perhaps the great communist intellectual Louis Althusser who best understood the benefits that Marxists could derive from cybernetics. Althusser had a very particular understanding of the impasse into which communism had stumbled under first Lenin and then Stalin. For him, it was not that socialism had been taken hostage by autocratic and sociopathic leaders who had to be eliminated so that a 'socialism with a human face' could emerge, as Jean-Paul Sartre thought; he insisted that, on the contrary, it had remained the prisoner of a still too 'humanistic' vision of politics. Althusser did not mean that Mao or Stalin had been oversentimental leaders, but that by giving in to the cult of personality, they had betrayed Marx's fundamental idea that communism must emancipate itself from all masters. According to Althusser, the only way to save communism was to entirely reject the 'metaphysics of the subject' by embracing the idea that history administers itself without any help from humans, that it is a 'subjectless process'.

The communism he developed is presented as a 'structure': a system with several ways in, with no centre and no overall command, endowed with multiple subsystems articulated to one another in an 'overdetermined' way, meaning that they are not determined 'unilaterally' but by means of loops that ensure their consistency. This Marxism, which Althusser called 'structural', is in fact inspired by the feedback and loops of cybernetics. And indeed there is a connection: Claude Lévi-Strauss, one of the founders of structuralism, had attended the multidisciplinary Macy Conferences in New York, which during the 1940s and '50s brought together the leading lights in postwar cybernetics. Jacques Lacan, another structuralist, was also a computer enthusiast. Noam Chomsky used programming languages to develop his work in linguistics on generative grammar.

Did this influence the pioneering information technology projects that the USSR carried out from the 1960s onward? It doesn't seem likely. But there is no doubt that, after Stalin's ideological condemnation of computer science as an 'anti-revolutionary American science', which for a long time weighed upon socialists, and which even now explains their continuing mistrust of the information society, Khrushchev understood the benefits of cybernetics, especially for planning, in similar terms. Where up until that point economic data had been gathered by hand and transmitted to Gosplan for cross-comparison, the prospect of being able to generalize and automate data collection was sufficiently attractive for the Party to finance a national computer network project, OGAS, based on 20,000 data-harvesting units installed in factories.[2] This would have been an interesting rejoinder to Hayek's criticism, in his 1945 article on 'The Use of Knowledge in Society', that Soviet planning was doomed to fail because of its inability to collect as much information as the market can on the fair price of commodities.[3] And although ultimately the project did not come to fruition in a country still too marked by Chekist paranoia, it was operational in Allende's Chile in the 1970s. Designed by an eccentric cybernetics researcher named Stafford Beer (who drove a limousine and smoked cigars), the Cybersyn (Cybernetic Synchronization) project consisted in collecting data from factories and transmitting it by telex to a command centre where a computer was responsible for automatically ensuring the systemic stability of the economy.[4]

Certainly, Cybersyn was very rudimentary, and above all it was ultra-centralized, so one wonders what would have happened if, instead of disposing of it following his *coup d'état*, General Pinochet had made use of it to monitor and silence his opponents. But when in the 1970s advances in the miniaturization of electronic components indicated that a myriad of personal computers could replace the large, unwieldy calculation machines with which Wiener and Beer were familiar, it became possible to conceptualize the first truly decentralized control systems that prefigured Bitcoin.

Stewart Brand, the visionary founder of a collective that assembled itself around the *Whole Earth Catalog*, a journal aimed at bringing together engineers, biologists, poets and political activists, was one of those to have understood that computers were not just supercalculators but advanced tools for 'communication' and therefore potentially 'communism' – two words that audibly share an identical root, the 'common'. By allowing people to talk to each other instantly all over the globe, they were destined to make the world into that 'global village' promised by Marshall McLuhan, and ultimately, by relieving humanity of the burden of mechanical work, they would bring about a New Cockaigne; by teaching us to speak the secret language of life itself, the language of DNA, they would make it possible to invent a new nature where, as the poet Richard Brautigan wrote, 'we are free of our labors / and joined back to nature, / returned to our mammal / brothers and sisters / and all watched over / by machines of loving grace'.[5]

With these promises, and in a world that was

cruelly in need of a bit of optimism – between the collapse of 'actually existing socialism', the beginnings of anguish over climate change, and the crimes of American democracy in Vietnam – the magazine published by this group to disseminate its ideas met with immediate success. The *Whole Earth Catalog* very quickly began to circulate widely in the countercultural world, but also among engineers and programmers – so much so that, according to the American historian Fred Turner,[6] this cybercommunist or 'cybercommunalist'[7] utopia played a significant part in shaping the information society in which we live today. It was there in the background of the invention of the Internet as a 'web'. It paved the way for social networks and their culture of free access. It motivated open-source projects such as the Linux operating system and the Wikipedia foundation. Above all, it is the reason why Silicon Valley still believes it is entrusted with an almost divine evangelistic mission that brooks no protest.

But of course, in this case too, the dream did not quite deliver. Fifty years after the techno-hippy dream, we can see quite clearly that the Cybernetic International has done no better than its ancestor, the Socialist International.

The Internet has also, more than anything else, ended up enriching banks, multinational telecommunications companies, retail giants, the military-industrial complex, and the antennae of the control society. Unlikely monopolies have developed in commerce and advertising that threaten the very democracy the Internet was supposedly going to foster. The walls between peoples rose back up almost as fast as they had fallen. Intercultural dialogue has deteriorated into identitarian conflict. Social networks have become algorithmic bubbles in which indignant voices speak to themselves as in an echo chamber. According to some, the main achievement of the 'sharing economy' consists in delivering free labour to 'cognitive capitalism'.[8] Even genome technologies have denatured the 'cybernetic ecology' dreamed of by the poet. In short, decentralization has become recentralized, so that more and more left-wing intellectuals now see computers as a plague and call for the Internet to be dismantled, for the Big Four tech companies to be nationalized, and for Big Data monopolies to be broken up just as the antitrust laws once broke up Big Oil.[9]

Despite all of this, the informational utopia

lived on. The cyberpunks of the 1980s, in particular, argued that the problem of the Internet was only that it was decentralized *in the wrong way*. Alexander Galloway's book *Protocol* shows, in the words of the subtitle, *How Control Exists after Decentralization*,[10] demonstrating that techno-hippies had been a little too quick to forget that the Internet is based on centralized cable and server logistics that allow malicious actors to swallow up all available data and for data monopolies to be created. In 1998 John Perry Barlow proclaimed a 'Declaration of Cyberspace Independence' in protest against ICANN's control of the Internet. In 2002 media theorist McKenzie Wark wrote a *Hacker Manifesto* that called for the disrupting of information flows. It is those cyberpunks who developed all kinds of tools to resist the control society and digital capitalism – technologies to anonymize connections (Tor or VPNs), to encrypt private messaging (PGP) and to create peer-to-peer networks (P2P) – who really paved the way for Bitcoin.

But it might be said that the cyberpunks themselves were not as successful as they hoped in avoiding the trap, already denounced by Marx, of thinking that an information 'market' would empower its users. Indeed, in some cases they did not so much change the structure of the Internet as create an even larger opening for capitalism. After all, it's only one step from the Dark Web to tax havens. Between the pirating of movies, mailboxes, various assorted leaks and drugs trafficking, it is difficult to know what separates a pirate from a corporate boss, unless it's just a question of scale. Nevertheless, the cyberpunks did pave the way for the *cypherpunks* who, in turn, managed to shift the entire Internet into a new dimension.

3

From Democratic Centralism to Decentralized Consensus

Bitcoin is a protocol for generating consensus in a decentralized way. It is in this sense that it is a deeply political technology, even before it is an economic and financial one. And it is in this sense, especially, that Bitcoin is Marx's dream become reality.

Before the blockchain, it was necessary to choose between consensus and decentralization. Either you were on the side of anarchy or you were on the side of the control society. Achieving consensus presupposed that a central body had to control and validate the opinions of community members. For example, it is the assessor's job to collect and count ballots to ensure that no one has voted twice. And banks play a similar role:

when a payment is made by cheque or card, or even by PayPal, the issuing bank and the creditor bank agree to write in their accounting ledgers that the amount X is to be deleted from Bank A's book and transferred to Bank B's book, and this once and only once, otherwise 'double payments' would make fraudulent transactions possible.

By its very nature, this third party that validates collective expression must be a trusted third party, otherwise the whole process is flawed. But it can also be corrupt and can misuse consensus to its own advantage. There is no shortage of examples of this, as Marx and Hayek argued, as did Luther and Rousseau before them. Hence the importance of Satoshi Nakamoto's discovery that a software protocol makes it possible, under certain very specific conditions, to do without any such trusted third parties.

The discovery was made when Satoshi succeeded in resolving a game theory problem known as the Byzantine Generals Problem.[1] The problem in question is to determine whether it is possible for several generals surrounding a city with their troops to agree on a common strategy, attack or retreat, given the following conditions: (1) an uncoordinated attack or retreat would be a disaster; (2) the generals are separated from each other, so that they cannot vote unanimously by show of hands, but can only send messages to each other; (3) the messengers they use to communicate with each other can get lost and their messages never arrive; and (4) some generals are corrupt or have been turned by the enemy, and may send contradictory messages ('beat a retreat' *and* 'attack'). In other words, the problem is how to ensure that an agreement (i.e., consensus) can be reached between several people when no one of them in particular can be relied upon (i.e., when there is no centralized control body).

Satoshi's solution to the problem proceeded in three stages. He first stated (1) that a voting register should be accessible to all generals and must be included with every message they send to each other. To ensure the uniqueness of the votes recorded in this register, Satoshi then indicated (2) that a vote in favour of an option ('attack' or 'retreat') should be based on 'proof of uniqueness'. Since it could not be a simple signature at the bottom of a parchment (too easy to fake), he imagined that it would instead be a kind of 'puzzle'. Each general should have to solve a cryptogram the solution to which would constitute his 'signature'. But since the resolution of the cryptogram would require a certain amount of time, he added that the voting process must take place within a limited timeframe – precisely equal to the time it takes to solve the puzzle – so that it would be impossible to solve two of them and therefore to 'sign' two contradictory messages. Finally, Satoshi solved the last problem, which was to make sure that everyone had the same voting register. To do this, he (3) obliged each general to 'chain' his vote with that of the next general, so that a modification of any element in the chain would change the whole register.

Replacing the generals with computers, and their votes with information that they exchange with each other, we get Bitcoin. The 'generals' are computers organized in a peer-to-peer (P2P) network. They share a ledger that circulates, containing all the messages they send to each other, and which they can only write to if they provide, along with their message, a 'proof of work' which consists in finding the solution to a cryptogram that takes ten minutes to crack (providing this solution is called 'mining'). Each session of 'voting' forms a time-stamped block that is chained to the previous one (hence 'blockchain') after checking that the new addition on the register is legal. This verification is performed by 'nodes' that cannot read the block information (since it is protected by a cryptogram) but can tell whether the chain of blocks is properly integrated.

What is strictly speaking called a bitcoin[2] is the receipt given to a miner (e.g., the person or entity using the computer to crack the cryptograms, ensuring the blockchain is secured from double writing) each time a new block is created on the chain, although this way of expressing it is not quite right, since the coin is in fact a *bit* of the block itself, the writing space it contains. It is a right to draw on the encapsulated information contained in the block. And that's how it can have a value: owning write permission on the blockchain is like owning an http:// address on the web or a parking space in a building. The value of the parking space is greater the more residents there are who want to park, and the less room that is still available to create new parking spaces.[3]

The combination of miners, users and nodes constitutes Bitcoin: a protocol for exchanging information that is perfectly transparent (everyone has a copy of the register in which it is written), decentralized (no one has control over it), and yet unforgeable (validated by proofs of work), indecipherable (the information is encrypted) and inviolable (the integrity of the chain is constantly checked).

Bitcoin is often described as a 'trustless exchange'. This is only true because it is possible to have faith in the entire protocol and its actors, a faith that stems from the possibility of 'verifying' what each person does. Miners can trust Bitcoin because they can supervise coders whose work provides them with a fixed income. Users can trust Bitcoin because they can monitor miners and make sure they comply with the written rules of the coders they host in the nodes of the network. Coders (who write the programs in use) can trust Bitcoin because they know that the miners ensure the reliability of the network by using energy to secure it.

In fact, coders, users and miners form a community that divides up the legislative (code), executive (users) and judiciary (validation) powers of Bitcoin. So Bitcoin is a kind of state – and it comes with its own constitution. Nothing can be done without these three powers agreeing to change the protocol. If agreement is not reached between them, though, the chain can fork, if 51 per cent of a given class wants to go in one direction at all costs. But precisely, this will come at a cost. Value is destroyed with each fork, and trust degraded. Building consensus is therefore crucial, and remains a fundamental activity of those who describe themselves as belonging to the 'Bitcoin community'.[4]

It is therefore a mistake to retain from 'decentralized consensus' only the word 'decentralized', as cryptoanarchists want to; the word 'consensus' is far more important. The value of a bitcoin is inseparable from the network that supports it. Bitcoin is a 'social relationship', in Marxist terms. Indeed, that's all it is. It crystallizes the energy of the social body that produces it. The central authority that the protocol abolishes – the bank, the state – is in fact distributed throughout the body that bears it: it is the coercive implementation of consensus at all levels of society. This is literally nothing but a successful version of Soviet 'democratic centralism' (where 'centralism' now means 'consensus' and 'democratic' now means 'decentralized').

4

Fully Automated Blockchain Communism

One of the pioneers of cryptocurrency, Naval Ravikant, has summed up very well the way in which the blockchain works, halfway between market and state.[1]

According to him, there are several types of collective organizations, which can be ranked according to their ability to balance 'inclusion' with 'selection'. The most selective are the most optimal, but also the least inclusive – one example would be the Protestant Trusts that lie at the origin of modern banking, and which brought together a few carefully selected Partners; universities are another, more broadly welcoming but still very meritocratic. At the other end of the scale are the most open networks: democracies, for example. They are inefficient because trust between parties is low and individuals are very disparate. But what is lost in efficiency is gained in inclusiveness, through a mass effect. Between these two extremes there is a network that has found a way to combine mass effects and meritocracy: the market. A market is by definition open to all, but there is an entry requirement, namely 'risk', which makes it both open and selective. A market is *elitarian* – both elitist and egalitarian, a combination so formidable that markets have gradually become more powerful than governments. But markets have one weakness: they are solely financial, and so involvement in them is a mercenary affair. No one enters a market out of the goodness of their heart. A proof of this is that, at the slightest sign of risk, everyone scatters, and the markets are shaken by violent crises. No *affectio societatis* regulates the markets. Companies can try to engender this to some extent by giving their employees an investment in the company's results or by creating an effective corporate culture, but their power is limited. Fear of unemployment is much more effective. Paradoxically, markets are therefore more fragile than they seem, and their fragility threatens everyone; at any moment they can come undone. That's why they need the state: to force otherwise reluctant citizens to enlist in the market.

A blockchain doesn't have that kind of problem. It rewards the commitment of its members, their attachment to the common. It makes *affectio societatis* into a market. It values loyalty. It doesn't just invite you to exchange on a network, but to make the network the very object of the exchange. On the blockchain we are not mercenaries or pirates; on the contrary, we are civil servants, network civil servants. All the more so in that this network *is* us, it belongs to us. A blockchain thus combines the openness of democracy with the efficiency of the meritocratic market. Beyond mere money alone, it makes of democracy itself a labour that deserves some kind of compensation. In this way it reverses the balance of power between public and private and paves the way for communism.

Politicians like to compare the nation to a company, especially politicians who have been a 'success' in business and who want to make voters think that they will make their country and their businesses prosper. This metaphor is misleading, insofar as no one is willing to die for their company, and death is the cornerstone of any society, as Hegel saw clearly. Nations are neither companies nor markets. They are social organizations, assemblies of co-owners. If a building burns down, all its inhabitants perish with it. If a resident has a contagious disease and the other residents fail to provide care, they will all die too. Indeed, it was only when cholera,[2] which decimated the lumpenproletariat population living in the poverty-stricken districts of central Paris in the nineteenth century, became a threat to the upper class living in the west of the city that the first public health policies were promulgated and the bourgeoisie finally understood the importance of paying their taxes. A nation therefore already functions intuitively as a blockchain. The community rewards the contributions of citizens who take risks for the common good by giving them tax breaks that are the equivalent of tokens. The salaries paid to civil servants are another way of rewarding society's 'miners'. As on the blockchain, the teacher, postman or soldier is paid in (treasury) bonds in exchange for their work in the service of the entire community. Similarly, political parties and unions receive public money for the votes they have received: they are in some sense paid to lead the community, like the manager of a co-ownership housing complex.

But this blockchainization of the state stops halfway. We are never paid to vote, for example, even though voting is just as important to the community as the work of a union or a party, indeed arguably even more fundamental. Voting is considered not as a job but as a duty, or even as a gift for which the citizen should be grateful rather than expecting a reward (and this has long been the case in so-called 'censal' democracies). Sorting garbage, helping to clean up a beach soiled by an oil spill, participating in educational and social activities: these activities are also unpaid. In short, there is complete disregard for community life, for all of the activities that Amartya Sen calls 'empowering' and which allow us to move from a negative freedom, where the state appears only as a burden and where citizens are clients or users, to a positive freedom, where everyone feels part of a whole and is respected as such.

The reason for this may seem obvious. Who would pay for all these activities, if not the citizens themselves? Wouldn't it be like giving yourself your own money? Wouldn't it be just one more tax, a form of redistribution unsustainable for the state budget? As the supporters of modern monetary theory (MMT) show, this is not the case if it is paid for by sovereign money issued by the state (which thus writes a cheque to itself), still less so if it is issued by a blockchain: just as MMT teaches us that taxes are not the source of state wealth, but a means to regulate the overflows of money it injects into the economy, so blockchain is a system in which value is produced by the money that is 'mined', while taxes are just a way to counteract inflation. Hence anyone doing work for the community would be paid in the digital currency they 'mine' and taxes would actually give these 'civic bonuses' a nominal value, since they could be used to pay for services between members of the national blockchain, outside the traditional monetary circuit. Any state would therefore have (at least) two currencies: its trade currency and a sovereign blockchain, the national currency of civic services – as was the case for centuries.[3] The state would thus acquire a currency that went 'from each according to his ability, to each according to his needs', to paraphrase Marx.

Better still, the state could levy taxes on a sovereign blockchain. Contrary to what cryptoanarchists argue, although Bitcoin makes it possible (in theory) to escape the control of tax services, in fact a blockchain that captures financial exchanges perfectly centralizes the collection of taxes (albeit not on a property but on transactions, which happens to be much more efficient). We may imagine that if one day states themselves begin to mine Bitcoin, the bitcoins and transaction fees that miners now collect on any exchanged bitcoin would be collected by the entire community. This global 'Tobin e tax' would be the equivalent of a universal housing tax, serving to keep the national infrastructure in good condition. It would be an ideal candidate with which to finance an unconditional basic income, even if Marxists do not like the principle very much.[4] This would be what activist Aaron Bastani calls 'Fully Automated Luxury Communism'.[5]

Part II

Collective Appropriation of the Means of Monetary Production

5

Thermocommunism

According to traditional leftist intellectuals, the other reason why techno-hippies failed to build the 'Global Village' is not because the Internet wasn't sufficiently decentralized, but because it is used only for communication. Capitalism can only be overcome if the means of production are taken over. As Gilles Deleuze said:

One can of course see how each kind of society corresponds to a particular kind of machine – with simple mechanical machines corresponding to sovereign societies, thermodynamic machines to disciplinary societies, cybernetic machines and computers to control societies. But the machines don't explain anything, you have to analyse the collective apparatuses of which the machines are just one component. Compared with the approaching forms of ceaseless control in open sites, we may come to see the harshest confinement as part of a wonderful happy past. The quest for 'universals of communication' ought to make us shudder.[1]

The fact is that, if the state is privatized, according to Marx this is not just because ill-intentioned people misuse power to their own advantage, it is because the productive apparatus is already privatized, and its owners hold the state to ransom so as to increase their profits. So Marx did not just think the Party should be given the responsibility of destroying the state, but that it should also be given the task of abolishing private ownership of the means of production.

This is obviously another point that strongly distinguishes communism from cryptoanarchism. The socialization of the means of production is libertarianism's bugbear. Not for nothing does the first 'piece' of Bitcoin, the Genesis Block, carry an inscription taken from *The Times* headline of 3 January 2009: 'The Times 03/Jan/2009 Chancellor on brink of second bailout for banks'. This refers to the fact that after the 2009 subprime crisis, which saw banks bailed out using public funds, Satoshi feared that a new banking crisis would see them being bailed out by private funds – a 'bail-in' that would constitute a direct drain on individuals' bank accounts. So Bitcoin was designed to protect private savings from the voracity of governments, even if it meant participating in a collective effort, and above all even if it meant 'socializing' losses.

However, once again, perhaps on this point libertarians may just be Marxists who don't yet realize it, because unlike the http protocol, not only is the Bitcoin protocol a vehicle for 'communication', it conveys value, it is *money*, and therefore a powerful lever for economic action; but what Bitcoin proposes in order to avoid the arbitrary power of banks is a 'collective appropriation of the means of monetary production', so that one might wonder whether it is not the very instrument communism needed in order to be truly realized, even if Marx himself would probably have found it difficult to believe.

Because Marx didn't really think about money when he considered the socialization of the means of production. In fact, he never took any particular interest in the issue of money. He never believed that monetary policy alone could bring about a communist society, unlike Proudhon, for example, who argued that the emancipation of the proletariat depended on the emancipation of the currency issued by bourgeois banks, or even on the total abolition of money; or the Englishman Robert Owen, who invented the first complementary currency for workers. Marx described these alternative currencies as 'no more "money" than a theatre ticket is',[2] he saw them as Monopoly money that made no difference to the relationship of domination between bosses and workers, or to the process of extracting surplus value upon which capital accumulation is based. On the contrary, he thought that Proudhon and his friends were succumbing to the fascination of a 'fetish', that they were falling into the capitalist trap of 'gold fever'.

Marx was very proud of his discovery that money is an abstraction, because value does not exist in itself. Only labour exists. It is only the labour congealed in a commodity that endows it with value. This thesis is partly rooted in Marx's philosophical reflections on the limits of Hegelian idealism and his desire to found, by contrast, a 'materialist' thought, a philosophy for which, whereas 'philosophers have only *interpreted* the world, in various ways, the point is to *change* it', as the famous phrase from *The German Ideology* says. But it has other sources. Today we are more aware that it also owes something to Marx's familiarity with the scientists of his time, especially those who invented the science of energy, 'thermodynamics', associated with the first steam engines.[3] Marx was a fascinated contemporary of the works of Sadi Carnot, Rudolf Clausius, Herman von Helmholtz and James Prescott Joule, from which there emerged the stipulation that all forms of work come from 'energy' and the popularization of the idea that the whole universe, and perhaps even life itself, therefore obeys two startlingly simple principles: the conservation of energy (nothing is lost, everything is transformed) and the dissipation of the working capacity of energy (nothing is lost, but everything is diluted).

Marxism is in large part precisely an extension of the laws of thermodynamics to society and the economy. Indeed, this is what makes it still relevant, against all odds. Before Marx, economists had largely borrowed scientific models from the physics of so-called 'equilibrium' dynamic systems, such as the solar system as described by Newton, governed by the deterministic laws of action and reaction.[4] These laws, which assume that societies achieve their optimum state in perfect conditions of exchange between supply and demand, are the basis of the so-called neo-classical school of economics. However, we now know that this model is flawed, as evidenced by the inability to prevent every crisis that has occurred over the past two centuries. History is not a clock whose cuckoo comes out at a fixed time; it is an internal combustion engine, and humans do not 'act' or 'react' rationally to their environment. With Marx, and perhaps especially with Engels,[5] the economy was for the first time adequately understood on the model of so-called 'far from equilibrium' dynamic systems – those described by thermodynamics, characterized by violent and disordered shocks between molecules and unpredictable state transitions. This is the model to which the notion of 'dialectical materialism' essentially refers: a science of moving matter, of the chaotic. Conversely, it became possible to set out the terms of a 'scientific' socialism: it would consist in the task of eliminating injustice from society by taking control of the thermodynamics of the economy, just as engineers had succeeded in taking control of steam engines.

The abolition of private property follows from this. For the fact is that thermodynamics also teaches us that it is necessary to intervene in the operations of these machines. Otherwise, they are subject to 'decreasing efficiency': a steam engine that produces a certain amount of work the first time will produce a little less the next time, and so on, until it runs out. Once again, Marx transposed this observation, originally made by the French physicist Sadi Carnot, to society: the work of the proletariat is similar to the heat that boils water; some of this heat produces 'free energy', i.e. energy useful for making things – the activation of a piston in the case of the steam engine, the production of value in the case of capitalism; and some of this work releases heat that can be reintroduced into the next cycle to fire it up again; finally, there is another part of this work that simply dissipates, reducing the power available for the next cycle unless more coal is put into the boiler, i.e. unless more is demanded of the workers. This is what Marx calls the 'law of the tendency of the rate of profit to fall', and it is this law that explains the alienation and grinding down of the proletariat by big capital.

The reasons why steam engines suffer from decreasing efficiency have only been properly understood recently, however. It was clear that some kind of mysterious force condemned dynamic systems to death by exhaustion (this is the meaning of the second principle of thermodynamics), but the first principle of thermodynamics states that 'energy is conserved' and that nothing is lost. It was therefore tempting to think that the energy that goes missing after each cycle was somehow 'stolen' and that if a way could be found to recover it, the secret of perpetual motion would be found. This is partly what Marx thought, and we know this all the more so since Engels damaged the reputation of 'scientific socialism' by challenging the validity of the second principle of thermodynamics. For Marx and Engels, the first law, that of energy conservation, took precedence over the second. They imagined that someone – in this case the capitalist – was 'stealing' some of the missing energy, which, if reintroduced into the cycle, would allow the economy to perform at its best. This stolen energy being the 'surplus value' extracted off the backs of the proletarians, they came to the conclusion that the only way to give it back to them was to abolish private property.

But Marx was wrong on this point. While it's certainly true that there is a drain on capital income during the economic cycle and that this injustice creates immense tensions in the social 'cylinder', to the point where it can sometimes implode, it is not the cause of its diminishing returns. As Ludwig Boltzmann showed after Carnot, it is the result of energy that is still there, but in such a degraded form that it can no longer be used for work. In other words, it is not that the energy is stolen, but that its form is altered in such a way that it can no longer be useful for anything. Along the way, it loses something that Marx didn't know existed – and for good reason, since it wouldn't be well understood until long after his death: it loses *information*.

The dissipation of information over a thermo-dynamic cycle refers to the fact that temperature differences even out over time, and the ability of energy to do work depends upon inequalities in temperature. The greater the difference between the temperature inside the cylinder and the temperature outside, the more information there is, and the more intense the work produced. Conversely, as the cylinder warms the air around it, temperature differences are evened out and it becomes more and more difficult to produce them. In short, and to use Marx's own term, in thermodynamics there can be no *perpetuum mobile*.[6] In economics as in physics, there is a kind of 'accursed share', to use a phrase employed by Georges Bataille, precisely in a thermodynamic sense.[7]

In fact, the productive nature of temperature differences is the reason why capitalism likes to put the social body 'under tension'. It has understood that it can extract more work from the proletariat if it subjects it to the desire to access the upper levels of society. Conversely, the remedy that Marx proposed for inequalities, the abolition of private property, is very counter-productive, since it results in an acceleration of the equalization of temperature levels, and will therefore make the extraction of free energy ever more difficult.

Of course, it will be said that not everything in social matters can be reduced to temperature differences. This is the meaning of Engels's rather dry retort to a Russian physicist, Sergei Podolinski, who thought he was doing useful socialist work by calculating the amount of watts consumed and produced per worker per hour. Humans are symbolic beings, not energy machines. They can compensate for their equal temperatures (in this case, equalities of property) by inequalities in culture, ideas and points of view. However, Marx pretended not to know that even immaterial differences must be determined in objects, goods, 'properties', and therefore also in differences in properties, if they are not to remain entirely abstract and to become diluted in turn into a homogeneous tepid soup. This suggests a possible hypothesis about the decline of the Soviet Union: that it succumbed to accelerated heat-death,[8] while, conversely, the prosperity of the liberal bloc during the same period owes to the fact that it allowed and even encouraged the formation of a market of symbolic differences, including for example the fashion, music and leisure industries.

So perhaps if Marx had had access to the concept of information, he would have thought very differently about overcoming capitalism, and maybe he would have thought precisely in terms of money, which is never anything other than a measure of *economic information*.

6

The Monetary Institutions of Capitalism

From a thermodynamic point of view, there is only one realistic response to the increase in a system's entropy: *opening it up*. This can sometimes be done by consuming the 'accursed share', as Bataille understood very well: a car engine manages to keep going thanks to the exhaust pipe, which allows it to export its entropy to the outside, preserving the temperature differential at the same level inside. Sometimes it can be done by importing information into the thermal system, by recreating order, regulating temperature differences. In the case of the car engine, this is the role played by the cooling system, which recovers some of the dissipated heat and uses it to cool the engine using a fluid with refrigerating properties.

The capitalist instinctively gets this. Every time he colonizes a new territory, he exports his entropy. Conversely, every time he invests the money he has earned to modernize the production facilities or to train his employees rather than sitting on his surplus value, he imports information. He improves 'productivity', meaning that he minimizes energy dissipation in favour of free energy production. By achieving the same value creation at a constant energy, he solves the problem of decreasing efficiency. Fixed capital acts as an 'entropy sensor', and this is the secret of the miraculous survival of capitalism. This is how it manages to resolve the contradictions that should have destroyed it long ago. Capitalism is a spontaneous information economy.

Marx also vaguely foresaw this. Obviously, he understood the role of capitalist imperialism. He was also fascinated by the dynamics of investment, which is proof that under certain conditions it is possible to reverse the law of diminishing returns, that famous second law of thermodynamics, the one that condemns any dynamic system to exhaustion and death – meaning that perhaps Engels may have been right to question it. Human work is capable of 'negentropy'. Evolution can be 'creative', as Henri Bergson said.[1] 'The evolution of species', as established by Charles Darwin in 1859, itself designates the way in which species constantly increase their own productivity so as to increase the amount of free energy they can produce from the same amount of available energy.

Now, what makes this miracle possible is money – capital, insofar as it is information. In order to really grasp the situation, then, Marxism must include money in its considerations. In particular, it should aim to prevent the privatization of money, rather than abolishing private property, because it is the privatization of *access to investment* that is ultimately responsible for the existence of private property, as the Austrian economist Joseph Schumpeter, a great admirer of Marx, has shown. It is this that causes the inefficiency of markets, and therefore explains their tendency to secrete the state.[2]

For Schumpeter, capitalism is inseparable from investment, and therefore from credit (which provides access to the money needed for investment), and therefore from money. Capitalism must create money permanently in order to support its growth, because to lend money to an entrepreneur is essentially to create it: banks do not lend money they already have in their account (fortunately, since otherwise it would be lost to everyone in the case of bankruptcy); they create it, and this all the more easily given that the fictitious money is meant to be repaid, and therefore to disappear, apart from the loan interest, which remains in the bank's pocket and is very real. This explains why a country's money supply tends to grow over time. Conversely, when the money runs out, owing to bankers' lack of confidence in the ability of entrepreneurs to repay their debts, a liquidity crunch causes the economy to contract. When this happens, central banks intervene by injecting liquidity into the banking system, as has been done in recent years with the policy of 'quantitative easing'.

The problem, says Schumpeter, is that even if entrepreneurs start off equal when they access investment, and the market is therefore efficient, incestuous relationships arise very quickly between entrepreneurs and their bankers. As a company grows, its financing needs become greater, to the point where it can jeopardize the very bank that provides for those needs. The bank is no longer in a position to exercise judgement and risk assessment, but becomes dependent on the company, rather than the other way around. And companies can then influence banks' choices, leading to the risk that they no longer lend to the competition, and become a source of inequality in access to investment.

Similarly, a powerful entrepreneur can influence the central bank's interest rate policy, which will make it more difficult to access investment again, favouring established incomes at the expense of new entrants. This was what happened in the late 1970s when Fed Chairman Paul Volcker, US President Ronald Reagan and British Prime Minister Margaret Thatcher raised interest rates to almost 20 per cent. Certainly, Volcker's move was intended to stop real inflation stemming from the twin oil shocks of 1973 and 1979. But Reagan's and Thatcher's intentions were not so clear. They were mostly afraid that the wealthy class had been losing continuous ground to the working class since the 1950s, and they took the opportunity of the oil shocks to bend the curve in favour of the former. Indeed, the effect of this manoeuvre was radical: at the very moment when the non-owning classes (and developing countries) had just multiplied their exposure to debt, they found themselves squeezed by higher bills, which excluded them permanently from access to property, and even bankrupted some,[3] but also shut off their access to investment and entrepreneurship, while on the other hand the propertied classes became richer by lending their money.[4] At the end of what amounts to a real 'coup',[5] capital had therefore taken control of society.

The often rather vaguely employed notion of the 'financialization' of capitalism really refers to this phenomenon of the *privatisation of currency issuance* for personal enrichment that began in the 1980s. But a system like this cannot be artificially sustained indefinitely. You can't block access to money without paying the price at some point. As Schumpeter has shown, economic cycles are punctuated by crises, one of the causes of which is precisely this: the privatization of investment. In 1992, for the first time, then in 2000, and then again in 2008, debt levels became unsustainable, money flows dried up, and banks were forced to appeal to governments to rescue them. Household debt that had become bank debt now became government debt, and since governments are financed by households, it was financed by printing yet more money, up until the most recent injection of billions of dollars and euros into banks. Banks that, in turn, had not stopped lending to entrepreneurs, and lent only to those who already had money (sometimes the same people who were at the controls of the political levers of the economy), so that this money was only used to buy even more real estate, gold and unproductive goods, rather than to fuel a new cycle of growth.[6] No doubt the Weimar hyperinflation of the 1930s is once again waiting in the wings. In 2015, Greece was forced to devalue its own labour force, since it was unable to devalue its own currency. Venezuela, Argentina and Brazil seem to be stuck in a deleterious inflationary spiral, while Turkey is now falling into one. Gold and real estate, but also stock markets, stuffed full of free money, are now overheating. The populist movements that are growing all over the world are the consequence of the increasingly evident and ever greater proletarianization of the middle classes to which this policy leads.

As mentioned above, Bitcoin was invented to combat the risk of systemic crisis posed by this privatization of monetary issuance. And once more, this is why we believe that it should be understood in the context of a communist economics.

7

Fool's Gold

Satoshi's intention in creating Bitcoin was not only to allow savers to protect their nest eggs from government intervention in the event of a further financial crisis; he also wanted to address the causes of the crisis. Because blockchain produces consensus, it can endow information with the qualities of energy, in the sense that it makes it possible to produce and transport *non-duplicable information*. In fact, whereas passing on energy normally means losing it while passing on information only means sharing it, on a blockchain, passing on information means losing it too. So a *bit* can become a *coin*, it can have a rarity that gives it a price, a price that is all the greater in that this *bit-coin*, which has all the qualities of energy, also has those of information in terms of speed of transmission and fungibility. The blockchain is therefore able to automate the printing of money and to replace a bank or even a central bank.

It must be admitted however that, when he designed Bitcoin, Satoshi didn't have Marx or Schumpeter in mind, but Hayek. For Hayek claimed that it would only be possible to put an end to the dysfunctions of liberalism if currency was freed from the supervision of politicians, states and even central banks, even though they were designed on his own model of the 'council of wise men', which he himself had come to realize was ultimately unsatisfactory. Satoshi therefore conceived Bitcoin not only as a currency without an issuer, but as a 'hard currency' – a currency whose issuance is predictable and based on strict rules, as opposed to the currency created by the whim of credit banks, with the power vested in them to declare 'let there be currency!', which gives it the nickname '*fiat* money'. The number of bitcoins produced is capped at 21 million units, and their rate of issuance is planned in advance on the model of a kind of 'digital gold' whose total number of mines and extraction capacity are already known.

Libertarians have understood this well: they see Bitcoin as the saviour they have been awaiting for decades, come to destroy the international monetary system and bring it into line with their fantasy of monetary (or other) 'hardness'. Since it is of better quality than the currencies in circulation (i.e., since it is deflationary), they think it will compete with them and gradually replace them until it becomes a new gold standard, a 'Bitcoin standard'[1] that will put an end to the undeserved supremacy of the dollar, established as an international settlement currency since the Bretton Woods agreements of 1944, and which has not only been phoney money since the end of the parity between gold and the dollar decreed by Nixon in 1971, but is also a tyrant's currency used to put pressure on anyone who doesn't support American foreign policy. At the same time, they believe that Bitcoin will make wars impossible to finance (because they are always financed by printing money) and even that it will clean up the terrible moral disorder that prevails in the consumer society. In their view, and following Hayek, the hedonism that corrodes the foundations of society finds its origin in debt and easy credit. A deflationary currency discourages consumption, since the value of the money you have grows with every passing day that you don't spend it, and a currency that prohibits the creation of money from fractional reserves discourages credit, since the only way to borrow money is to take it from existing reserves that have been hard-earned by saving. Bitcoin is thus intended to encourage the virtues of endurance, continence and frugality that characterize strong men and solid societies, unlike all those 'soft currencies' associated with periods of moral decadence, military clashes and economic decline.

This vision of the world is not a completely unsympathetic one, since it expresses views that are more socialist-leaning than it realizes. Indeed, a German socialist economist, Silvio Gesell, was the first to theorize currencies of this kind, which he called 'free currencies'.[2] But we can't be so sure that such a thing is viable, or even that it would not produce the exact opposite of the intended effect. For example, it's simply false to claim that there was always prosperity and peace during periods when the gold standard or some other monetary standard was in force. If the 1914 war broke out when the gold standard was in full effect, it was not because England was exempt from it, but precisely because the gold standard had created imperialist tensions throughout the world. And the 1929 crisis, or at least the way it went from a simple stock market crisis to a huge depression, can also be seen as a problem linked to the gold standard.

The problem with the gold standard is that it limits the liquidity available to markets. In other words, it makes it extremely difficult to access credit, especially when a credit crunch occurs, as in 1929. In fact, the gold standard is the apex of the privatization of money. Only affiliates of the bank who enjoy the trust of the partners are entitled to lines of credit. Everyone else is locked out. So much so that the height of the gold standard, the nineteenth century, was also the era when colossal industrial fortunes were made against a backdrop of rampant poverty. Without the invention of the steam engine, which made huge productivity gains possible, and which had nothing to do with the gold standard, the Victorian century would have been an economic disaster, in addition to the social disaster it undoubtedly was.

Besides, even the gold standard is a false promise. It cannot prevent the creation of money, which is endogenous to economic activity, as Schumpeter showed. We have to be able to create money. And if an entrepreneur can't access the credit he needs in gold bars, he will invent it in shell necklaces. Indeed, the gold standard era coincided with a completely anarchic multiplication of means of payment far more dangerous than fractional reserves, since they were entirely unregulated, as documented, for example, by Balzac, whose characters are always inventing new ways to accumulate debts (and not to honour them): from 'bills of exchange' to 'drafts', 'pledges' and 'promissory notes'. In China today, the unofficial debt market exceeds the official debt market. Shadow banking threatens the stability of the world far more than central banks. And even the gold market is not immune: after all, what are gold derivatives, futures and exchange-traded funds if not fractional reserves that have allowed their content and value to be diluted so as to extract more money and liquidity?

Actually existing money – the money in our pockets – is only the tiniest tip of the monetary iceberg. Money is really money only because it has the potential to be more. For it is precisely always possible – and this is perhaps the most fascinating thing about money – to create money from nothing. It is enough for two people to agree on what money is for it to exist (provided that the thing used obeys certain rules, first and foremost that it is reasonably difficult to counterfeit). After all, that's what makes it possible for bitcoins to have a value. The reason for this miracle is that money is like the paradoxes of formal logic identified by Bertrand Russell: it is self-referential. It is a content (the number of pieces I have in my pocket), but it can also be the form of this content (the price I have to pay in order to have this number of pieces in my pocket, or the number of additional pieces that have to be paid in order to have them). In other words, money fixes the price of goods, but it also has a price itself – a price that is stated in money.[3] Now, as Kurt Gödel showed in regard to Russell's paradoxes, it is impossible to prevent paradoxes from being created. One may well dream of a 'clean' formal axiomatic system in which reflexive and non-reflexive operations are clearly separated, but there will always be undecidable problems. One can always dream of giving pure form to money, but there will always be another, impure money that will overflow that form. The idea that the value of money can be fixed forever is simply infantile.

Satoshi was therefore wrong on this point when he built Bitcoin. He certainly made a great store of value out of it, but in no way a great means of exchange, let alone a means of investment. However, if in doing so he succumbed to the original sin that forbids any return to the Garden of Eden of value, he nevertheless allowed us a glimpse of what he could have done to avoid it: since money is necessary, since it is constantly being created, and since the problem is not that there is too much of it but that access to the money that exists is always made more difficult by those who possess it, who profit from it to fill their own pockets, distort competition and manipulate market prices, he should have totally freed up its creation, rather than hopelessly trying to force things.

8

Everyone's a Banker

When they dreamed of the Internet in the 1970s, cybercommunalists believed that a unified global information network would allow everyone to access the same high-quality information. What happened was the exact opposite. The Internet has led to a proliferation of fragmented, poor quality and even outright manipulated information sources. Inside their algorithmic bubbles, everyone consumes the information that recommendation programmes advise them to look at based on what they already like. In fact, the Internet has not given rise to a global media, but has enabled everyone to become their own media. Kanye West's tweets now count for almost as much as a *Washington Post* editorial.

The blockchain may be headed for the same fate. Today, cryptoanarchists believe that a single currency of exceptional quality will prevail across the entire surface of the planet: Bitcoin, a new international standard. But what is more likely is that there will be thousands of them, most of which will be of the same poor quality as the majority of online media. The blockchain allows everyone to become their own banker, say bitcoiners – which is true, provided they understand the full implications of the word: it doesn't mean that everyone keeps their valuables in their own safe; it means that everyone can now coin money, like a commercial bank or a sovereign state. Certainly, probably only one financial exchange protocol will survive into the future (the Bitcoin protocol, like the http protocol, not to be confused with the bitcoins that circulate on it, which are only the element that serves to secure it). But there will be as many currencies carried on this protocol as there are web pages.[1] And maybe that's the most communist outcome of all.

Since the creation of Bitcoin, 'altcoins' have multiplied ever faster (there are now more than 2,000 of them). Most of these altcoins are modi-

fied versions of Bitcoin with added features, such
as the ability to put lines of code in blocks so as
to execute smart contracts (Ethereum), or better
anonymization of transactions (Monero). Some
of them involve a modification of the chain's
security (proof of stake, proof of address, proof
of existence . . .). Others propose a variant of
the blockchain blocks (hashgraphs). But others
are tokens issued by companies in exchange for
future products (Initial Coin Offerings, ICOs, or
Initial Exchange Offerings, IEOs). Here, instead
of issuing shares or going into debt with a bank,
a company goes into debt with its customers. The
tokens work like gift certificates or pre-purchased
airmiles that will be deducted from a future
purchase.

This last model of altcoin is particularly interesting insofar as it offers an escape route from the
Schumpeterian investment problem prevented by
the incestuous links between bankers and investors. Instead of asking a bank to create money so
as to give it credit, at the risk of being rejected or
being offered unfair terms determined by existing
monopolies, then being exposed to interest rate
fluctuations over which they have no control, entrepreneurs can instead create their own currency.

The creation of money no longer involves bank debt, just the spontaneous generation of money, provided that the issuer has a community willing to buy it (in the same way that one only receives likes if one delivers a rich information content to one's followers). And this also eliminates the need to pay interest to the bank, which further limits the artificial inflation of the money supply and the risk of monetary depreciation.[2]

Such variants are possible – for example, the Petro launched by the Venezuelan government, which took advantage of the fact that the country produces energy to create an energy currency free of the petrodollar system, which essentially legitimates the Fed's excessive issuance of dollars by backing it up with a source of real value. In *The World Set Free*, written in 1913, H. G. Wells, who had already prophesied a future 'global brain' – of which the Internet is a direct descendant – wrote that pegging the exchange rate to gold made no sense. Instead, it was necessary to create energy accounting units. Each currency would be exchangeable for energy to be consumed. Petro comes close to this kind of energy currency, far more useful to our world than a return to the gold standard.

Another variant is *stablecoins*. It is clear that people, just like states, need a stable currency in which to make their payments. But it is doubtful whether Bitcoin can be used for this, not so much because of its volatility, which will decrease over time, as because of its lack of liquidity, since the number of bitcoins is capped. One of two things is going to have to happen: either the Bitcoin community will vote to lift this cap and encode a new algorithm that could, for example, index the number of bitcoins in circulation to global energy consumption, based on Frederick Soddy's energy currency model,[3] meaning that the Bitcoin money supply would track global liquidity needs (and would also contract during a recession), making it a kind of super-Petro or super-Bancor;[4] or it will fall to a stablecoin to serve as a payment currency. This could be issued by a state consortium such as the IMF, in the form of a digital SDR.[5] Or it could be issued at the initiative of a foundation such as Libra, Facebook's recently announced cryptocurrency. This is not exactly money creation, since Libra is backed by reserves, but in theory nothing would prevent Facebook from offering credit on a fractional reserve basis, so that billions of people who currently have no access to banks (especially in developing countries) could obtain credit via Facebook. If Facebook also made Libra a token currency with which to pay its most active users, all the major principles of a mini-state would be in place. Admittedly, civil liberties would not be guaranteed there as on Bitcoin, but in real-world use there is always some kind of compromise between freedom and functionality.

On Ethereum, many decentralized finance (DeFi) tools already make it possible to lend money on the blockchain. Tether, the most popular stablecoin in the ecosystem, is already suspected of operating a fractional reserve system, albeit without the knowledge of its users.[6] Finally, we can even imagine 'currency curren-cies' that would just be smart contracts ensuring interoperability between currencies, like futures but without the need to be backed by a reference currency such as the dollar.[7]

It is difficult to imagine the revolutionary con-sequences of this modernized version of universal priesthood (where 'everyone is a banker' replaces 'everyone is a priest'), which we could just as easily call, in imitation of Marx, 'the collective appropriation of the means of monetary production'. It's too early to say. The altcoin market has undergone a global collapse in recent years, having suffered from a number of frauds reminiscent of the gold rush era. Price volatility is out of control, with fortunes sometimes made and lost in a single day. It would obviously be crazy to put all your savings into crypto today. Far from causing a situation of anarchy, the bet is that, in the long run, the long-awaited stability will come, and that the international monetary system will therefore benefit, with the state no longer required to intervene in its traditional role as a pyromaniac firefighter. In particular, the dollar would lose its role as a benchmark currency. The *lex americana* would no longer be able to impose itself upon the world.

As economist Bernard Lietaer has said, an economy is like an ecosystem: if you plant only one species of tree, you gain in speed and productivity, but you run the risk of losing everything in the event of a fungal disease or fire. Conversely, if you maintain forest biodiversity, you lose in productivity but ensure much greater resistance to disasters. Currencies are like trees.[8] Today they are all intertwined, they are all issued in the same way, by central banks, dominated by the dollar, and they all serve the same purpose: to buy goods, pay taxes and repay debts. Every financial crisis is therefore a contagious crisis that threatens to take the entire monetary system with it. If there were different types of currency, a variety of currencies, a proliferation of currencies even, all issued differently and for different uses, circulating at different speeds, then financial crises would not automatically turn into currency crises. Monetary biodiversity would protect the economy.

Better still, nature already has a kind of monetary system that works on this model. Thermodynamicist François Roddier reminds us that one of the mechanisms our body uses to regulate itself is the parallel assembly of hormones in opposite phases. The sympathetic nervous system takes care of the activity phases and the parasympathetic nervous system takes care of the sleep phase, insulin represses sugar and glucagon expresses it. An economy with just two currencies, hot and cold, would find itself in the same configuration, an antagonistic equilibrium.[9]

Part III

A New International

9

Collectivist Intelligence

Marx missed the role that money plays in the economy because he missed the role that information plays in thermodynamics. However, his project to regulate the thermal machine of society remains relevant today.

We know that it is the fate of all thermodynamic systems to go through cycles of 'creative destruction' (Schumpeter), which can be painful and which in the past, as perhaps in our immediate present, have resulted in tyrants coming to power. These cycles are due to a phenomenon that physicists call the 'Red Queen Paradox', named after the character in *Alice in Wonderland*: you have to run ever faster to stay in the same place.[1] In fact, there is always a point in the history of any system where the rate at which the environment degrades exceeds the rate at which information can be imported. In the metabolism, this occurs when the rate of cell renewal no longer manages to keep pace with the rate set by oxidation. On an evolutionary scale, it occurs when the rate of the adaptation of species cannot keep up with the degradation of resources: in the Cretaceous era, large size was an advantage in the struggle to secure food, but it became a disadvantage when food became scarce, and small mammals supplanted dinosaurs.

In an economy, the increase in productivity also always reaches a limit, which Marx correctly identified: it is the cost of innovation, which increases the cost of fixed capital to the point where it ceases to be profitable.[2] Economic activity grows exponentially with each innovation cycle, so that the overall energy required also increases, even though each individual requires less energy; and since the rate of profit begins to decline again as soon as all competitors close the technology gap,[3] soon the whole planet has to be cultivated, in every last corner. The system seems as if it is going to blow and, in fact, we have the crises to show that it does so at regular intervals, as if it had to open the release valve to let off excess steam.

In far-from-equilibrium dynamic systems, then, we tend to see cycles of intense growth followed by episodes of depression, crisis and even collapse. This is described as 'punctuated equilibrium' (Stephen Jay Gould) or self-organization around a 'critical point' (Per Bak). After a period of growth and maturation (spring and summer) there comes decline and hibernation (autumn and winter). Animals, humans and societies all experience these moments of collapse: death (the metabolic cycle), sleep (the circadian cycle), economic crises (Kondratieff cycles) . . .

Possibly, these cycles harbour a kind of fatalistic truth. The universe has been operating like this since the Big Bang, which may itself have been the result of a thermodynamic imbalance in the 'fluctuations of the quantum vacuum'.[4] Evolution is a struggle for life punctuated by episodes of mass extinction. We may even wonder whether it's worth trying to fight it. After all, if we talk about 'creative destruction', it is because after each destruction a better world emerges. Thermodynamic cycles are not just the 'eternal return of the same' that terrified Nietzsche.[5]

Each new cycle comes out of the previous crisis stronger.[6] Even freedom is made possible by imbalance, as explained by the great expert in far-from-equilibrium thermodynamic systems, Ilya Prigogine.[7] In stable dynamic systems, those of neoclassical harmonies, Newtonian orbits and Walrasian 'optima', there is no room for novelty. Disorder is the condition of possibility for freedom, life and mind.

Without going so far as to want to abolish this source of freedom, we can nevertheless imagine destruction taking a form other than the destruction of economies and people. It is precisely the destruction of effigies rather than, and in the place of, people that is the great marker of civilization. In the struggle between master and slave, the cycle of violence is interrupted by the emergence of language, which makes it possible to invent the law and to transfer violence between individuals to a symbolic institution that will have a monopoly over this violence by means of rules. As Hegel said: 'It is an excessive tenderness for the world to keep contradiction away from it, to transfer it to spirit instead, to reason, and to leave it there unresolved.'[8]

In 1858, the young Marx ventured a hypothesis

along these lines which economist Yann Moulier Boutang describes as 'stupefying', given how ahead of its time and how deeply in contradiction with the fundamentals of Marxism it was.[9] In essence, Marx argues that it is possible that the most sacred pillar of his economic theory, the 'law of value' – the law that value must be equal to accumulated work – may in the near future be invalidated by the production of surplus value based on what he does not call information, but is something close to it: the general quantity of 'intelligence' accumulated in society.

This so-called 'General Intellect' hypothesis is based on a simple idea: that with the increase in productivity, there must come a time when machines become so powerful that people are freed up for tasks other than the production of goods. But if they use this free time to produce more information, by devoting themselves to study and invention, then it is possible to further increase productivity, so that a virtuous circle is set in motion: as wealth increases, collective intelligence increases, which increases overall wealth, etc. 'Capital increasingly takes the form of an objective and neutral power created by the collective human brain.'[10]

Today this hypothesis is confirmed by two thermodynamic phenomena of which Marx knew nothing. The first relates to the issue of equality. The war between species and competition between humans is not life's last word. Biological evolutionism in no way justifies the theories of 'social evolutionism' espoused by Charles Darwin's cousin Francis Galton, who believed it was valid to say that 'survival of the fittest' was the natural condition of the economy since it was the natural condition of life, and that the theory of evolution therefore justified the existence of capitalism and inequality. In fact, phenomena of mutual assistance and cooperation are more frequent as cycles follow one another. We see this as early as the appearance of the first plasmas, atomic groups in which all particles synchronize electromagnetically. We see it with bacterial colonies, which work together. We see it in social insects such as bees and in the symbiotic associations between plants and animals. Finally, we see it with the hypersocial animals that we ourselves are, in our construction of huge communities: companies, unions, parties, cities, nations, etc. This growing tendency towards associativity does not come from nowhere. It is due to the fact that energy is gradually being replaced by information. But one of the properties of information is that, unlike energy, it does not get used up as it is passed from hand to hand. Energy is lost when it's passed on, whereas information can be shared out into as many copies as there are people to receive it.[11] This means that animals that have the same genome (the same genetic information) have an innate feeling of being part of the same species; they spontaneously form a global brain.[12] Similarly, humans who share the same language form groups capable of collective intelligence. The more information accumulated in the cycle, the more communication there is between its parts, and therefore, in a sense, the more 'communism'.

The second phenomenon concerns adaptation. With each cycle, the mutation rate increases. If the human species is now the dominant species on earth, it is because, whereas the rate of adaptation of small mammals remained limited by the rate of mutation of the information stored in their genomes, humanity has found a way to mutate faster than they do by storing information in our brains; it is easier to change mental habits than to change genes. Our inventiveness enables us to resist famines, bad weather and changes in climate, even extreme ones, much more effectively than animals do. However, the rate of mutation of information is potentially infinite; it can reach a point where the speed at which the environment degrades will never be greater than the speed at which information is imported, which is the speed of light. Certainly, our brains are not capable of reaching this speed.[13] But the speed of computers can far exceed our capabilities. Computers can increase the speed of information transmission to the limit speed of light.

Although no amount of increase in information in a given society is sufficient in itself to achieve socialism, it is possible to imagine under what circumstances a socialist condition might be achieved: on condition that the importation of information reaches a kind of 'escape velocity' or 'critical mass' that irreversibly and instantly triggers the transfer of ownership of capital into equal hands. Having reached this limit, capitalism would not collapse as long as it turned into communism, just as water passes from a liquid to a gaseous state when heated above 100 degrees Celsius. In short, communism would be the 'infinite speed of thought', as Deleuze said.[14]

10

The Resurrection of Nature

The most common criticism of communism is that it is a form of ideology, or even a religion. Didn't Marx popularize the dream of a popular 'international', and even an Edenic reconciliation between man and nature? Didn't he believe in a history freed from evil? Unfortunately, utopias are bloody precisely because they are only utopias and must therefore force reality to conform to their fantasy, at the risk of breaking it when it resists. In contrast, the crypto milieu sees itself as pragmatic. It believes only in what works. And it believes it is bringing about a peaceful revolution because it is made up only of engineers who have no philosophical axe to grind.

And yet, at least according to the theory of

'General Intellect', Marxism's success depends directly upon the progress of science, technology and, in particular, Moore's law on the performance of computer processors. And the blockchain, too – so it may be that crypto is more metaphysical, or even more religious, than it wants to acknowledge. And for good reason. Doesn't it also have a totalizing ambition to rival that of Marxism? Because it is a computer protocol, it is part of the great history of logic and ontology that is consummated by computer science. In fact, it is the blockchain alone that can fulfil Marx's dream of thinking at 'infinite speed'.

This already becomes evident once the uses of blockchain are expanded beyond money. The blockchain is not strictly a banking ledger but a universal ledger, and what's more a digital and therefore programmable ledger, which can potentially serve as a framework for all kinds of contracts, not just financial contracts.

As a universal registry, a blockchain can house *proofs of existence*. Just as the bank guarantees proof of a transaction, so the state usually guarantees proof of a person's existence and identity through their government records. A blockchain can provide it just as efficiently, if not more so, and with

a more secure guarantee for those concerned –
we know what kind of state government files are
in, and how they are sometimes put to dubious
uses, since our data do not belong to us; we also
know how laborious it is to prove one's status in
the event of losing a passport or identity card,
especially when one has parents born abroad, in
countries whose records, like their currencies, are
subject to suspicion or may be destroyed. These
proofs of existence can be used as a general way to
securitize information: a photo 'timestamped' by
its owner or sender becomes unforgeable, offering a possible way to prevent the multiplication
of fake news, and particularly deep fakes.

Along the same lines, the blockchain can house
proofs of ownership. Today, notaries do this work
in the same way as banks, by reconciling ledgers
and giving it their imprimatur (with their stamp,
timed and dated). Tomorrow, the blockchain will
do the job for us. The same applies to copyright.
Or marriage certificates. The blockchain could
also be used to mechanize voting, with each voter
strictly identified and each vote recorded as a
transaction.

Finally, as a programmable currency, a blockchain can house *proofs of execution*. To do this, it

is sufficient to stipulate that payment X should be made only when event Y is observed to have taken place. This might relate to rentals between private individuals, insurance policies, futures contracts. In this capacity, the blockchain replaces the rental platform, the insurer, the lawyer. Ethereum, the blockchain developed by Vitalik Buterin, is now exploring this functionality. Ethereum is a blockchain specifically designed to house 'smart contracts'. Unlike Bitcoin, which (at the moment) only carries money, Ethereum is Turing-complete, which means that (in theory) it could be a carrier for any cryptocurrency, any automatic contract, and even any other blockchain.[1]

Ethereum thus demonstrates how the block-chain's ultimate vocation lies in *automating automation*. It is conceivable that, in the future, connected objects will exchange value tokens with one another independently of human intervention. The car will pay its own parking charge or toll – and in the event of unpaid bills or fines it will also be self-locking. When cars are autonomous, they will also pay for their own gas. Complex circuits of machines – already dubbed DAOs (decentralized autonomous organizations)

– will operate on the blockchain without human intermediaries. Better still, machines could replicate themselves on the blockchain: so long as they can earn money, they could spend it by ordering spare parts to repair themselves, or even replicas of themselves to which they could connect.[2] In this case, humans would end up serving the will of the machines rather than the other way around. Factory owners could be either machines or people, as could the workers.

Some will see all of this as a prefiguration of Skynet, the corporate network that escapes the control of its designers, Cyberdyne Systems, to give birth to the Terminator in James Cameron's eponymous film. But we could also see it as what Bruno Latour calls the 'parliament of things', which he hopes will abolish the distinction between humans and non-humans that has done so much damage to nature. The machines will be like a kind of artificial flora, a cognitive network of coral driven by their own interests, and which we will learn to live with symbiotically.

Marx wrote that communism is 'the true resolution of the strife between man and nature . . . the consummated oneness in substance of man and nature – the true resurrection of nature – the naturalism of man and the humanism of nature both brought to fulfilment'.[3] Here again, it may well be that crypto is the real solution to this strife.

II

Leviathan 2.0

The information circulating on the Internet today forms a web. The bitcoins that are exchanged on the blockchain form a tree. Each transaction is like a twig that winds outward from another and extends it. Bitcoin is a Deleuzian 'rhizome': not only a reticulated and branched organism (a simple decentralized network), but a *root* organism. This means, in particular, that there is not a hardware network on one side and information, software, on the other. It is made of what circulates on it. Its information constitutes its physical existence. Bitcoin is captive energy (the energy it takes to solve a puzzle), in the same way that a plant is captive energy, or DNA is captive energy.

Indeed, DNA exhibits surprising similarities

to blockchain. Cryptographer Ralph Merkle, inventor of the 'Merkle tree' that is part of Bitcoin's infrastructure, was the first to notice this.[1] The first similarity is that DNA does not exist once and for all. Its particularity is that it is replicated each time a new cell is created, so that DNA is present in each of them, just as it is present in each individual of an identical species. Even though each member is unique, it shares a common genetic structure, so that individuals can reproduce among themselves (they are fungible) and the death of an individual never jeopardizes the survival of the entire species. In other words, like the blockchain, DNA is a distributed ledger.

The second point that DNA and the blockchain have in common is the concept of the chain itself, or more precisely the idea of a protected, encrypted, enciphered chain. It is essential to life that the writing of DNA follow strict rules. Each molecule must be strictly allocated, the chains must be solid and, in order for replication to be accurate and reliable, it must not be possible for anyone to be able to write whatever they want. To make sure of this, DNA uses a *proof of work*: the immune system, whose function is to distinguish between self and non-self.

The membrane of a cell and the skin of a body are primary barriers that play this kind of role: they are the first to create a crypt within which life can replicate itself. Phagocytic cells are like internal customs officers, as are the white blood cells of the lymphatic system. In a general sense, cellular receptors play the same role (A cannot bond with C, or G with T). DNA's 'proof of work' is the energy it expends to create stable electromagnetic bonds between atoms. Likewise, not just any individual can modify the genome of the entire species to which they belong. As in the blockchain, you need a majority in order to create a fork. Individuals of a mutant species must either be the only ones to survive a shock in their environment or must multiply until they become a majority in order to fork the species. It is therefore natural selection that plays the role of consensus builder or proof of work.

Finally, the third point the blockchain has in common with life is what it allows us to do: smart contracts are like the mini-programmes of DNA that give rise to the organism as such, and to its differentiated organs. In the same way that a certain molecule is released under certain circumstances, so smart contracts control an operation according to an IF/THEN logic. An individual's genome is designed to execute a myriad of smart contracts instinctively and automatically. Here, it is not money that is the subject of transactions, it is information. Each individual processes the information he or she receives from their environment and reacts according to his or her own interests. And the reward for good behaviour (behaviour that benefits the whole species) is not a bitcoin, but the ability to reproduce, to replicate. Precisely, the purpose of life is the form of the chain itself – the act of building it – just as the value of Bitcoin depends entirely on the blockchain that supports it.

In fact, there is a kind of circularity between life and the blockchain. Not only do they resemble one another, but one leads to the other. If the aim of life is to replicate itself, it must find the most appropriate, solid, stable, but also fastest, form. Evolution therefore requires life forms to become increasingly cunning. Those that survive are the ones that replicate better and faster. And man has acquired a decisive skill in the form of language, which makes it possible to store and process information in an extraordinarily efficient way and free from the constraints of mortality – even more so with computer language. The invention of the computer is, in fact, part of the history of evolution. It is driven by life itself, looking for the best place to continue its work of replication. The blockchain therefore closes the loop by offering life the most stable and the fastest system with which to replicate itself.[2] Individuals do not own life, they are vehicles of a life that passes through them; they are the healthy carriers of that virus or 'selfish gene' that is life.[3] As a result, Bitcoin must be taken for what it is: not just a computer protocol, and not just a form of political organization in its own right, even one more efficient than previous forms, but a higher form of life, which has absorbed all the apparatuses for the self-preservation of life that have been tested over millions of years of evolution, to give birth to the most stable structure possible.

Political theory abounds in naturalistic metaphors. Aristotle compares the City to a living being. Paul says that the Church is the 'body of Christ'. Hegel refers to the State as a 'second nature'. Bitcoin takes this beyond mere metaphor. It is Leviathan. There is nothing to prevent us from considering it a person, a form of collective artificial intelligence, that common political body that Marx called for, or the global brain that Teilhard de Chardin spoke of.

It is commonly thought that machines will become intelligent when they are capable of consciousness. But this is to reverse cause and effect. Self-awareness precedes intelligence. As we have seen, it exists from the cellular level, in the form of the immune system, recognition and distinction between self and non-self. Consciousness is not a secondary cognitive faculty. If it were not already present at the origin of life, then no cognitive ability would be possible. What is needed in order for a machine to be conscious is not a more sophisticated programme, but, on the contrary, a very simple, very robust programme that allows it to distinguish between self and non-self. This protocol is precisely that of the blockchain – which suggests that Bitcoin will house the first artificial intelligence.

Of course, this doesn't mean that Bitcoin is an autonomous subject. At least not yet. But what is an autonomous subject? What is self-awareness? It is also a form of 'decentralized consensus'. It is the unity that results from the individual activity of all neurons. One of the most advanced explanatory hypotheses for the appearance of consciousness is that the electrical activity of motor neurons eventually forms a single electromagnetic wave that enters back into neural electrical activity to modify it and, above all, synchronize it.

Finally, let's imagine an ultimate blockchain, composed of myriad sidechains connected to an Internet of Things, itself composed of self-replicating machines, all 'mined' by a network of decentralized computers controlled by humans: the parent blockchain would contain the genetic endowment of all the individuals that make it up, and from this they would gain a sense of unity. Each one could say, 'I belong to the same species and I bear witness to it', by recognizing each part of this species as another version of itself (albeit in a non-verbal way). The parent blockchain would therefore exist within the milieu of all of these individuals, in the form of a diffuse feeling of 'Self'. Soon, a kind of body composed by the interaction between whole and parts would emerge, a body made of instructions, of rules: a language. Alexander von Humboldt said that language is similar to a living organism. It is also quite similar to a blockchain: the language is only forked if a majority of speakers agree to it. In language, evolution plays the same role as proof of work in the context of life. To speak the language of one's species is literally to speak the language that *is* one's species, to speak the molecular language that is DNA. To represent this to ourselves, it is enough to imagine an organism 'consuming' the whole species in question, so that this species now lives inside it, like a virus, that it lodges itself somewhere, in what will become its skull for example: here we have the prototype of a brain. Each individual of the species continues to live their life, but they are now a neuron, and thought is the result of the work of the neurons performing their species. In this sense, thinking, also, is a body. And this body is a proto-consciousness. In this way, then, we can imagine that our destiny is to become the neural network of the new life form that Bitcoin will be.

12

Living Currency

'A spectre is haunting Europe', said Marx. Alas, today it is the spectre of fascism. As capitalism completes the great cycle of growth that began after the Second World War, as GDP stagnates and profits threaten to fall, what are euphemistically called 'populist' parties are trying to repeat the trick that worked so well for them in the 1930s: instrumentalizing the 'ragged proletariat' in order to continue making money from the very *dismantling of the world*.

Trotsky described fascism as a mutation of capitalism that occurs when it reaches the limit of its ability to reproduce. This limit can take two forms: in periods of growth it is generated by the demands of the middle classes, who insist on participating in the fruits of development, demands that result in a decrease in the margins of the haute bourgeoisie; in periods of crisis, it comes about when the productive apparatus reaches such a stage of overproduction that the only solution is to liquidate stock. In both cases, the haute bourgeoisie is forced to break its natural alliance with the petty bourgeoisie if it wants to survive, and, since it is too numerically weak to rule alone, it must forge a new alliance with those whom Marx and Engels called the 'déclassé petty bourgeoisie' and the 'sub-proletariat' in order to take the middle class in a pincer movement. And that's where we are today. Make no mistake about it, the 'collapse' promised by a new large-scale financial crisis combined with global ecological crisis is now part of capitalism's plan. Some, now, are waiting for it, and want it to happen, in the hope that they will be able to profit from the chaos it will wreak.

Millenarianism is not the only abiding obsession within the crypto milieu. But whatever they say, bitcoiners are no match for the extreme form of 'disaster capitalism' that is on its way. They must face facts: their money will be taken from them at gunpoint, along with the gun they bought with which to defend themselves, as well as the self-sufficient house with its vegetable garden and panic room. No one will be able to fight the paramilitary militias of the mafia state that will take control of the infrastructure when the time comes.

The only solution is to act now before it is late, by rediscovering what made Marxism the most exciting political movement of its time: its Promethean dimension. Marx believed that, although there were no limits to the challenges facing us, with a knowledge of the laws of society, life and the universe, the vocation of humanity is to make the whole world its home and to transform nature into an extension of itself.

Today, however, this dimension of political action is generally deplored. With neither nature nor society doing particularly well, some think that the 'totalizing' ambitions that Marxism shared with fascism and capitalism may even be the cause of the disaster that afflicts us, and that therefore it is urgent to deconstruct the very concept of 'control', to become humble before nature again, and above all to no longer touch Mother Earth.

The truth is that neither the land nor the

economy is 'magical', and that to believe otherwise is just as deeply reactionary as the claim that Adam Smith's 'invisible hand' should be allowed free rein over markets. The earth and the economy are dissipative systems subject to the laws of thermodynamics. Indeed, were this not the case, we wouldn't even be able to conceive of the idea of 'ecology', and there would be no climate science. In fact, ecology and socialism have a shared origin, and in this respect they must be considered as twin political movements, their joint aim being to control thermodynamic cycles. Is there any other choice? The population continues to grow, and with it economic growth, human needs and waste. Quite legitimately, the South is also demanding its share of progress.

Marx's only fault – but it is a major fault, with incalculable consequences – is to have known nothing of the complexity of thermodynamic cycles, in particular the role that information played in them, as discussed above. No one would dare say that we now have perfect mastery over them. There is still a lot of work to be done in order to fully understand them, and in particular, paradoxically, to understand that they will never be fully understood since they involve chaotic and random phenomena. Nevertheless, we are better at controlling them than in Marx's time. Thanks to computer technology, we know that it is not true that we should not act on an ecosystem at all because it is so sensitive to initial conditions that a small deviation can have immense effects on it ('the butterfly effect'). In fact, it is a particular characteristic of these systems that, once they are operational, they are quite insensitive to external actions. They fluctuate around a 'strange attractor' (fortunately so, otherwise we would have turned the earth to ashes long ago). So there is nothing essentially sacrilegious in the idea of intervening in the gaps between the system and its attractor. Indeed, in economics it has long been encouraged and widely practised, as central banks temper the cycles of growth and depression by tightening or loosening their interest rate policies. Similarly, our body uses hormones to regulate energy intake, and these hormones can be supplemented with chemical substitutes when they are lacking.

The fact is that money is just a factor in economic cycles. In a broad sense, money forms a part of all thermodynamic cycles, and in particular organic ones. In biology there is an 'energy currency' better known as ATP (adenosine triphosphate), comparable to cash.[1] It is ATP that converts and transports the energy produced by glucose oxidation. It's a universal means of payment operating between all the organs of any one body, and even between all living species, animals and plants. ATP is the cash of life. Like cash, it is manufactured in banks – mitochondria, which are protected, like a safe, by membranes, and have relative independence (they have their own distinct DNA). Like cash, it changes forms several times as it releases its energy, but continues to circulate. Spent cash always goes to the mitochondria, which recycle it and put it back into circulation (the ATP becomes ADP by releasing its energy, and then the ADP is 'recharged' into ATP). Finally, like cash, there need be only as much ATP as the body needs at any given time. Insulin plays the role of the interest rate, regulating blood sugar levels at all times so as to inhibit or activate the formation of ATP. Too much ATP causes diabetes and the formation of fat to store the excess; not enough gives us cramps. Like GDP, ATP increases as a function of metabolic activity.

Finance, in this context, does not necessarily

play a harmful role – quite the contrary. It also serves to capture entropy. It could be compared to the pancreas, which regulates insulin and sugar storage. In the first instance, it serves to protect against the risk that a reversal of fortune could deprive the given system of the money (or glucose) due to it. A farmer who buys a futures option on the price of wheat ensures that, if prices fall, he will still have enough to live on. Similarly, there can be such a thing as good debt. If for some reason an organization is not able to synthesize enough energy for an immediate effort it needs to make (an investment), it can borrow energy from another organization, which will lend it *modulo* enough interest to cover the risk of its running out. So long as there is no need to get into more debt to pay the interest on the debt, everything is fine. Neither is it a problem that finance is very complex and that its operations take place at lightning speed. After all, why would we expect the thermodynamics of societies to be less complex or slower than that of organisms?

We just have to make sure that activity and money never come uncoupled. Imagine, for example, if mitochondria were to mount a *coup d'état*, deciding that ATP should be used only for their own growth, not that of the body. This is what happens when banks no longer support investment but speculate on their own behalf. Or imagine if the ATP they produced began to have an increasingly low energy content, or even contained no energy at all (like counterfeit money), so that it became necessary to circulate more and more, until the blood system became saturated, unable to carry anything else, any oxygen or nutrients. This is the equivalent of inflation.

Cryptocurrencies enable the optimal adjustment of the relationship between money and activity by serving as a converter between information and energy. In this sense, they are an essential step in the evolution of our species, just as agriculture and livestock farming enabled us to control the cycle of natural reproduction during the Neolithic period. They are nothing less than the key to our future. Bitcoin is not just a currency, or even a regulator of social thermodynamics, it is the currency of life, it is 'living currency'.[2] Hence, blockchains allow us to imagine a future in which relations between us are no longer dictated by exploitation because they are mediated by 'dead' money, but become relations of symbiosis within an organism self-regulated by one or more energy currencies of opposite phases, and whose only limit to growth would be the speed of the mutation of information – i.e., the speed of light, the speed of the universe itself.

This ontological communism, this communism of substances, is ultimately what we could call *cryptocommunism*.

Conclusion: Cryptoletarians of All Countries

The Left has not yet really grasped the importance of the blockchain, let alone Bitcoin.[1] There are many reasons for this, some of which have been alluded to above: a political culture that discourages any curiosity about money, and financial innovation in general; a complicated relationship with computers and information, which privileges a relationship with energy instead; the failure of 1970s cybercommunalism; and finally, Satoshi Nakamoto's personal libertarian penchant, which for some situates Bitcoin *de facto* on the right.

A big mistake. If socialists are really looking for a way to overcome capitalism, to destroy the state, to advance the ecological cause, then this is where they should be – not participating in vain, vociferous protests against the financial system, or joining sit-ins on Wall Street, let alone waging war for 'social justice'.

Of course, no one would claim that the revolution will be as easy as just snapping our fingers. With every passing day the world seems more fragile. Every day brings us closer to the collapse of another country under the weight of its economic and ecological debt. Before it is possible to regain control of the 'energy currency' of the earth and of society, a great deal of contaminated water, and even blood, will have to flow under the bridge. Especially since there are still many problems to be solved in the meantime. To speak only of Bitcoin, it is still limited by the number of transactions it can process per second, its decentralization is threatened by mining multinationals, its market is plagued by insider trading and adulterated financial products, and its very use, which requires a minimal mastery of software tools, is threatened by the technological divide that still separates rich from poor.[4] It would be a total disaster if Bitcoin's openness resulted in a renewed and terrifying 'power to shun' and cut out its noncompliant users or, worse, imprisoned their sins forever in the immutable chains of block of the blockchain.

The Reformation gave rise to a 30-year-long civil war and hundreds of millions of deaths before the new spiritual order it brought to the West was established. The great revolutions were followed by almost a century of world conflict between progressives and those nostalgic for the old regime. Perhaps it is too much to expect that crypto, following these two historical upheavals and bringing them to completion, will be achieved painlessly.

But that only means that we must do everything we can to take it in hand and to hasten its movement. Cryptoletarians of all countries, unite!

Notes

Introduction: The Institution of Liberty

1 Jean-Louis Schefer, *L'Hostie profanée* (Paris: P.O.L, 2007).

2 See Harold J. Berman, *Law and Revolution II, The Impact of the Protestant Reformations on the Western Legal Tradition* (Cambridge, MA: Harvard University Press, 2006). In particular, Berman remarks upon the difference between the Anglo-Saxon and the Venetian banking models in this respect.

3 Needless to say, it didn't go down too well with the Catholic establishment. The king having taken a liking to the printing of paper money, inflation bankrupted France within five years.

4 Even more than it is a 'truth machine'. See Michael J. Casey and Paul Vigna, *The Truth Machine: The Blockchain and the Future of Everything* (New York: St. Martin's Press, 2018).

5 A belief that has fuelled the numerous reformations and revolutions that have continued to break out since the original Reformation and the French Revolution, on the basis there is always a 'purer' way of doing things.

Chapter 1   A State without Statism

1 Karl Marx and Frederick Engels, *The Communist Manifesto: A Modern Edition* (London: Verso, 2010), 61.
2 In his 1878 book *Anti-Duhring*.
3 Marx and Engels, *Communist Manifesto*, 62.
4 See Karl Marx, *Critique of Hegel's 'Philosophy of Right'* [1843], translated by Annette John and Joseph O'Malley (Cambridge: Cambridge University Press, 1977).
5 The Fed was created in 1913, but did not achieve real independence until 1978, notably under the influence of the work of Milton Friedman, who was close to Hayek. The independence of the US Supreme Court is quite obviously of a different order, as an institution that precedes neoliberalism by two centuries. Marx, however, always held that the doctrine of the separation of powers that justified its existence represented the very birth of the bourgeois state.

Chapter 2   Cybernetics and Governmentality

1 See Norbert Wiener, *The Human Use of Human Beings: Cybernetics and Society* (Cambridge, MA: Da Capo Press, 1988), first published in 1950.

2 B. Peters, *How Not to Network a Nation: The Uneasy History of the Soviet Internet* (Cambridge, MA: MIT Press, 2012).

3 According to Hayek, Soviet planning was doomed to failure because of its inability to collect as much information as markets on the needs and capabilities of the economy. Cf. Friedrich Hayek, 'The Use of Knowledge in Society', *American Economic Review* 35:4 (September 1945).

4 Eden Medina, *Cybernetic Revolutionaries: Technology and Politics in Allende's Chile* (Cambridge, MA: MIT Press, 2014).

5 From Richard Brautigan's 1967 poem 'All Watched Over by Machines of Loving Grace'.

6 Fred Turner, *From Counterculture to Cyberculture: Stewart Brand, the Whole Earth Network, and the Rise of Digital Utopianism* (Chicago, IL: University of Chicago Press, 2008).

7 Turner prefers this word, closer to the hippie spirit.

8 Yann Moulier-Boutang, *Cognitive Capitalism* (Cambridge: Polity, 2012).

9 We could cite Evgeny Morozov, Carmen Hermosillo, Bernard Stiegler, Richard Barbrook and the documentary filmmaker Adam Curtis, author of a successful TV documentary series that adopts the title of Brautigan's cybercommunalist poem 'All Watched Over by Machines of Loving Grace', but in a sense that soon proves to be deeply ironic.

10 See Alexander R. Galloway, *Protocol: How Control Exists after Decentralization* (Cambridge, MA: MIT Press, 2006).

Chapter 3   From Democratic Centralism to Decentralized Consensus

1 It should be noted that Satoshi had certain predecessors in finding this solution – among whom we could mention Adam Back, Nick Szabo, Wei Dai and, especially, Hal Finney.

2 With a small b, to distinguish them from the protocol itself, which we designate Bitcoin with a capital B.

3 However, the rarity of bitcoins of itself does not explain their value, which also lies in their usefulness. In *Bit by Bit: How P2P is Freeing the World* (ebook, Liberty.me, 2015), Jeffrey Tucker explains very well how the value of a bitcoin is linked to the 'friction' of the other payment methods it replaces. For example, if a money transfer from one country to another costs about $15, a bitcoin is 'worth' the $15 of friction saved by sending it from person Y to person W without incurring any bank commission. Where remittances are prohibited by governments that want to control exchange rates or even allow themselves to take money from their citizens' accounts in times of shortage, a bitcoin is 'worth' even more: it is worth the ban it allows them to bypass. It is worth the value attributed to being fully in control of your money, or even being allowed to have money, which is not the case for more than a billion people on the planet who are considered by banks to be unworthy of an account. Finally, in countries that manipulate the price of their currency by printing notes or changing interest rates, Bitcoin,

which is capped at 21 million units, has all the more value as money has less.

4 Among the charges laid against Bitcoin by critics such as the economist Yannis Varoufakis and the philosopher Jaya Klara Brekke is its lack of democratic governance. The faith it places in the algorithmic administration of the protocol, they argue, gives excessive power to coders, and even to miners, notwithstanding the fact that it carries the illusion of 'solving the political'; see Satoshi Nakamoto, *The White Paper* (Ignota, 2019). But an example of the power of collective deliberation that drives bitcoiners was given in 2016, when Bitcoin users (node owners to be precise) defeated a project, imposed centrally by miners, to increase block storage capacity after intense debate in the forums. As a result of actually *not* finding an agreement, Bitcoin 'forked' into two opposing branches, BTC and BHC. In other words, 'the political' was not solved by Bitcoin *per se*, but by the blockchain ecosystem, where it lives on in the form of natural 'species' competing for the truth. This is actually very close to the way Alan Turing himself thought undecidable (Gödelian) mathematical truths were to be solved by means of natural evolution (such as morphogenesis). And it could perfectly well be transposed to the scale of a monetary policy debate. If, for example, it were necessary to determine whether to increase the number of bitcoins in circulation, to permanently create a slight inflation, or even to tax transactions and redistribute the profits received, this would be done in the same way. A protocol such as

Tezos even proposes to host these debates 'on-chain' via decentralized methods for reaching consensus.

Chapter 4   Fully Automated Blockchain Communism

1 The thread is still available on the Twitter handle @ naval.
2 Note from the editor: this book was written before Covid-19.
3 Up until Napoleonic times, there were two currencies in the West: gold was used for international trade; an alloy, 'billon', was issued locally for local trade.
4 Marx thought that the state's role was not to be charitable, but to allow men to emancipate themselves by enjoying the fruits of their labour. In addition, Michel Foucault later showed how the state sometimes justifies increasing its control over individuals on the pretext of providing them with social benefits (the state has to know the condition of every citizen's health, their professional and family circumstances, etc.). So the inverse of a universal income could perhaps be a simple reduction in the cost of goods enabled by automation. Perhaps, in a communist society, things would be free, rather than life being subsidized. This may seem as unrealistic as the Lutheran promise of free grace, since it might be feared that, if everything is free, everything will be instantly devoured; but it could instead be the case that, by removing the fear of missing out, one also removes the gluttony that is the consequence of this fear. At least this was Marx's hope.

5 Aaron Bastani, *Fully Automated Luxury Communism* (London and New York: Verso, 2019).

Chapter 5   Thermocommunism

1 Gilles Deleuze, 'Control and Becoming', interview with Toni Negri, in *Negotiations 1972–1990*, translated by Martin Joughin (New York: Columbia University Press, 1990), 175.

2 Karl Marx, *Capital, Volume 1*, translated by Ben Fowkes (London: Penguin Classics, 1990), book one, part one, chapter 3, 'Money, or the Circulation of Commodities', 188.

3 Friedrich Engels, in particular, speaks explicitly of thermodynamics in his unfinished book *Dialectics of Nature*, which was the subject of intense correspondence with Marx, as pointed out by Daniel Bensaïd in *Marx l'Intempestif* (Paris: Fayard, 1995), by André Tosel in *Vers un communisme de la finitude* (Paris: Kimé, 1996), and by John Bellamy Foster in his *Marx's Ecology: Materialism and Nature* (New York: Monthly Review Press, 1999) and *Marx and the Earth* (New York: Brill, 2016).

4 This is the case with Marx's predecessors such as Adam Smith and David Ricardo, and even with some of his successors such as Leon Walras and John Maynard Keynes. See Peter Richmond, Jurgen Mimkes and Stefan Hutzler, *Econophysics & Physical Economics* (Oxford: Oxford University Press, 2013), the introduction in particular, along with the report written on the invitation of Bernard Lietaer's Club of Rome-EU

Chapter, *Pour un Système monétaire durable* (Paris: Odile Jacob, 2012).

5 Engels, who lived in Manchester, where Joule worked, kept abreast of the latest scientific news. He may have been the one who introduced Marx to thermodynamics, which he discusses at length in his *Dialectics of Nature*.

6 Money performs the function of 'a *perpetuum mobile* of circulation [of goods]': Marx, *Capital, Volume 1*, 'Money or the Circulation of Goods', 227.

7 Bataille aimed to write the first essay on economic thermodynamics, an idea that came to him after meeting nuclear physics researcher George Ambrosino, who in the 1930s introduced him to the science of energy and to the concept of 'entropy', which he then called the 'accursed share'. Thus his book *The Accursed Share* is subtitled 'An Essay on General Economics' or 'Economics on the Scale of the Universe'. See C. Mong-Hy, *Bataille cosmique: Du système de la nature à la nature de la culture* (Paris: Lignes, 2012). The first work on the same subject by a scientist (apart from Marx himself) would not be published until the 1970s: Nicholas Georgescu-Roegen's *The Entropy Law and the Economic Process* (Cambridge, MA: Harvard University Press, 1971).

8 Hayek and Ludwig Von Mises suggest that the levels of remuneration dictated by Gosplan, unrelated to the production of real value, along with price freezes, were technical causes of this 'informational' death. See Ludwig von Mises, 'Economic Calculation in the Socialist Commonwealth' (1920), https://mises.org/

library/economic-calculation-socialist-commonwealth; and Hayek, 'The Use of Knowledge in Society'.

Chapter 6   The Monetary Institutions of Capitalism

1 Marx, Bergson, Teilhard de Chardin, Bataille and even Freud: all intellectuals who have had to deal with thermodynamics have been both fascinated and troubled by the obvious fact that, although the second law of thermodynamics states that any dynamic system tends towards death or rest, nevertheless we see life and complexity proliferating. All were then prompted to invent some 'force' to explain the anomaly to themselves, whether 'work' (Marx), 'élan vital' (Bergson), 'universal love' (Teilhard) or a 'life instinct' (Freud). It was only when the difference between 'closed' and 'open' systems was established, i.e. when the concept of information was formalized, that it became possible to truly understand this paradox of self-organization.

2 Joseph Schumpeter, *Das Wesen des Geldes* (Göttingen: Vandehoeck & Ruprecht, 1970). See Odile Lakomski-Laguerre, *Les Institutions monétaires du capitalisme. La pensée économique de Joseph Schumpeter* (Paris: L'Harmattan, 2002).

3 The same thing happened at the international level: some indebted countries, such as Mexico, went bankrupt after 1979, which triggered the great cycle of monetary crises in emerging countries that continues to this day.

4 This is what is known as the 'Cantillon effect'.

5 The expression comes from Gérard Duménil and

Dominique Lévy: see their *The Crisis of Neoliberalism* (Cambridge, MA: Harvard University Press, 2010). The term 'neoliberalism', sometimes overused, could be employed more precisely as a name for this tipping point.

6 Frances Coppola, *The Case for People's Quantitative Easing* (Cambridge: Polity, 2019).

Chapter 7   Fool's Gold

1 See Saifedean Ammous, *The Bitcoin Standard: The Decentralized Alternative to Central Banking* (Hoboken, NJ: Wiley, 2018).

2 See Silvio Gesell, *The Natural Economic Order* [1916], translated by Philip Pye (London: Peter Owen, 1958).

3 Marx understood this, as we see clearly in Chapter 3 of *Capital*. He was the first to say that money is both a sign and a commodity (and not one or the other, as the two opposing economic schools of thought had previously argued).

Chapter 8   Everyone's a Banker

1 Tether transactions can already be carried out on Liquid, one of the 'sidechains' of Bitcoin. With 'atomic swaps' (a type of smart contract), bitcoins can also be converted into litecoins at will – and this is only the beginning.

2 It could be argued, as in the 1926 book *Wealth, Virtual Wealth and Debt* (London: Allen & Unwin), by chemist Frederick Soddy, one of the first people to have

explicitly linked thermodynamics to economics, that in fact interest is the cause of the only properly 'artificial' inflation of the money supply, compound interest especially. While it is legitimate for the money supply to increase with the influx of energy and information, the 'mathematical progression' of compound interest makes it grow at a completely incongruous rate, to the point where, at a certain moment, it will become physically impossible to produce enough wealth to repay it.

3 Soddy, *Wealth, Virtual Wealth and Debt*.

4 Bancor was the name of the supranational settlement currency proposed by Keynes. It had to be backed by a basket of currencies, but also by commodities. Hayek, also, imagined that his denationalized currency would be backed by commodities.

5 Special Drawing Right. See Alex Lipton, Thomas Hardjono and Alex Pentland, 'Digital Trade Coin: Towards a More Stable Digital Currency', *Royal Society Open Science* 5:7 (July 2018), https://royalsoci etypublishing.org/doi/full/10.1098/rsos.180155.

6 A recent investigation by the New York Attorney's Office revealed that Bitfinex, Tether's sister company, was lending USDTs to investors, when it was only supposed to put them into circulation in exchange for their dollar value. We will see whether it can be proven that this issuance without a cryptodollar counterpart also allowed it to manipulate Bitcoin's prices, which would be easy to do as it would be both judge and defendant in the case, since Bitfinex is also an exchange platform. It would be ironic if trust in Bitcoin were to

fall victim to the very thing it aimed to put a stop to, and Bitcoin had to be bailed out just as the Fed had to bail out the Eurodollar market.

7 Cf. Michael J. Casey, 'A Crypto Fix for a Broken International Monetary System', *Coindesk* (2 September 2019), https://www.coindesk.com/a-crypto-fix-for-a-broken-international-monetary-system.

8 Bernard Lietaer, *Halte à la toute-puissance des banques* (Paris: Odile Jacob, 2012).

9 François Roddier, *Thermodynamique de l'évolution: Un essai de thermo-bio-sociologie* (Paris: Parole, 2012).

Chapter 9   Collectivist Intelligence

1 The expression is that of biologist Leigh Van Valen. We could also call it a 'leopard paradox': 'If we want things to stay as they are, things will have to change', as Tancredi says in Giuseppe Tomasi di Lampedusa's novel *The Leopard*, translated by Archibald Colquhoun (London: Vintage, 2007).

2 See Michel Husson, 'Marx, Piketty et Aghion sur la productivité', *Contretemps* 5 (2010).

3 Karl Marx, *Capital, Volume 3*, translated by David Fernbach (London: Penguin Classics, 1991), part three, chapter 15: 'Development of the Law's Internal Contradictions'.

4 Ilya Prigogine, *The End of Certainty: Time, Chaos and the New Laws of Nature* (New York: The Free Press, 1997).

5 We know that Nietzsche had a keen interest in thermo-dynamics. His library contained the works of one of its

founders, Hermann von Helmholtz. Unfortunately, he went no further than the first law of thermodynamics, which utterly petrified him.

6 François Roddier compares this process to the metallurgical process of 'simulated annealing', where the defects in a metal are reduced by repeatedly melting it and allowing it to cool again. See Roddier, *Thermodynamique de l'évolution*.

7 Ilya Prigogine and Isabelle Stengers, *Order Out of Chaos: Man's New Dialogue with Nature* (London: Verso, 2018).

8 G. W. F. Hegel, *The Science of Logic*, translated by George Di Giovanni (Cambridge; Cambridge University Press, 2010), 201.

9 This hypothesis comes from the 'Fragment on Machines' in Marx's 1857–58 *General Introduction to the Critique of Political Economy* (also known as the *Grundrisse*). See Yann Moulier-Boutang, 'Marx et la stupéfiante hypothèse du *General Intellect*', *Alternatives Economiques*, dossier 109 (May 2018).

10 Ibid.

11 Once again see Roddier, *Thermodynamique de l'évolution*.

12 This doesn't mean they won't eat each other.

13 Our internal clock runs at the relatively low speed of 40Hzm and some of the information that circulates in our neurons does so at the speed of hormones released in an aqueous medium.

14 Gilles Deleuze, 'Des vitesses de la pensée', Course on Spinoza at Vincennes, 2 December 1980, http://www2.univ-paris8.fr/deleuze/article.php3?id_article=91.

Chapter 10   The Resurrection of Nature

1 There are many technical uncertainties surrounding Ethereum's ability to deliver on its promises. As for Bitcoin, it is only just beginning to implement the porting of secondary features (Lightning).

2 The lawyer Primavera de Filippi invented a robotic 'plantoid' that must collect bitcoins in order to reproduce.

3 Karl Marx, *Economic and Philosophic Manuscripts of 1844*, translated and edited by Martin Millagan (Mineola, NY: Dover, 2007), 102, 104.

Chapter 11   Leviathan 2.0

1 http://merkle.com/papers/DAOdemocracyDraft.pdf.

2 The only major difference between the two is that life operates by random mutations, while the blockchain operates by directed mutations, following a search for consensus. Only the future will tell whether a certain amount of chaos may have to be introduced into the blockchain too.

3 Richard Dawkins, *The Selfish Gene* (Oxford: Oxford University Press, 1976).

Chapter 12   Living Currency

1 The comparison is suggested by Roddier in *Thermodynamique de l'évolution*. One might wonder whether the Higgs boson, which endows each particle with mass but itself has no mass, is not also a kind of 'energy currency' at the level of elementary particles.

2 The expression is Pierre Klossowski's. See 'Living Currency', translated by Vernon Cisney, Nicolae Morar and Daniel W. Smith, in Pierre Klossowski, *Living Currency*, ed. Daniel W. Smith (London and New York: Bloomsbury, 2017).

Conclusion: Cryptoletarians of All Countries

1 There are exceptions, among which we could mention Brett Scott, Brian Massumi, Erik Bordelot and Baruch Gottlieb, founder of the Telekommunisten collective. Unfortunately, even when left-wing intellectuals pay attention to the blockchain, it is often to oppose existing implementations, especially those that are purely monetary, on the grounds that we must do other things with this technology than use it as money – as if money played no part in left-wing thought. We also see far too many projects for 'alternative blockchains' that are merely well-meaning chimeras with no basis in material reality and no revolutionary potential.

2 It should also be mentioned that Bitcoin has a well-known efficiency problem, although it is less dire than some say, at least in absolute terms. Calculations estimate the network's energy consumption was 15 TW/h in 2019, which is to be compared to the 2000 TW/h that air conditioning uses worldwide (see Marc Bevand, http://blog.zorinaq.com/serious-faults-in-beci/). It is in relative terms that the profligacy of the system is more apparent, in other words when that consumption is related to the number of transactions going through the network, but, hopefully, they should go up.